AutoCAD P&ID 2014 Tutorial

Online Instructor

This book may not be duplicated in any way without the express written consent of the publisher, except in the form of brief excerpts or quotations for the purpose of review. The information contained herein is for the personal use of the reader and may not be incorporated in any commercial programs, other books, database, or any kind of software without written consent of the publisher. Making copies of this book or any portion for purpose other than your own is a violation of copyright laws.

Limit of Liability/Disclaimer of Warranty:
The author and publisher make no representations or warranties with respect to the accuracy or completeness of the contents of this work and specifically disclaim all warranties, including without limitation warranties of fitness for a particular purpose. The advice and strategies contained herein may not be suitable for every situation. Neither the publisher nor the author shall be liable for damages arising here from.

Trademarks:
All brand names and product names used in this book are trademarks, registered trademarks, or trade names of their respective holders. The author and publisher is not associated with any product or vendor mentioned in this book.

Copyright © 2013 Online Instructor

All rights reserved.

ISBN: 1484858344
ISBN-13: 978-1484858349

DEDICATION

To my mother.

CONTENTS

1	Introduction	1
2	Tutorial 1	4
3	Tutorial 2	61
4	Exercise 1	72
5	Tutorial 3	77
6	Tutorial 4	90
7	Tutorial 5	102
8	Tutorial 6	121

Introduction

This book introduces you to AutoCAD P&ID 2014. It is used to create Piping and Instrumentation diagrams easily. It provides a symbol library that you can access from the tool palette. You can use these symbols to create P&ID's. You can use schematic lines to connect the equipment symbols. You can also display the flow directions.

AutoCAD P&ID is designed such a way that you work in a project environment, so that your work is ordered along with others working in the same project. You can also create reports using **AutoCAD Plant Report Creator**.

Scope of this Book

This book is written for students and engineers who are interested to learn AutoCAD P&ID 2014 for creating Piping and Instrumentation Diagrams (P&ID's).

This book provides a step-by-step approach for learning AutoCAD P&ID 2014. The topics include Creating a basic P&ID, Connecting P&ID's, Editing the drawing, Creating custom symbols, Managing Project Data, Generating reports, and Adding and defining new classes.

Tutorial 1 takes you through the creation of your first Piping and Instrumentation diagram. You create a simple P&ID.

Tutorial 2 teaches you to create a symbol and convert it into a P&ID object. It also explains how to connect P&ID's in a project using off-page connectors.

Tutorial 3 teaches you to manage the project data using the Data Manager. You will also learn to export and import the data related to a plant project.

Tutorial 4: In this tutorial, you will learn to edit a P&ID using various options available in AutoCAD P&ID.

Tutorial 5: In this tutorial, you will add a new class and assign a symbol to it.

Tutorial 6: In this tutorial, you will generate reports using **AutoCAD Plant Report Creator**.

Starting AutoCAD P&ID 2014

To start **AutoCAD P&ID 2014**, click the **AutoCAD P&ID 2014** icon on the Desktop. Altenatively, click **Start > All Programs > Autodesk > AutoCAD P&ID 2014 > AutoCAD P&ID 2014**.

AutoCAD P&ID User Interface

Various components of AutoCAD P&ID user interface are shown in figure below.

AutoCAD P&ID Tutorial

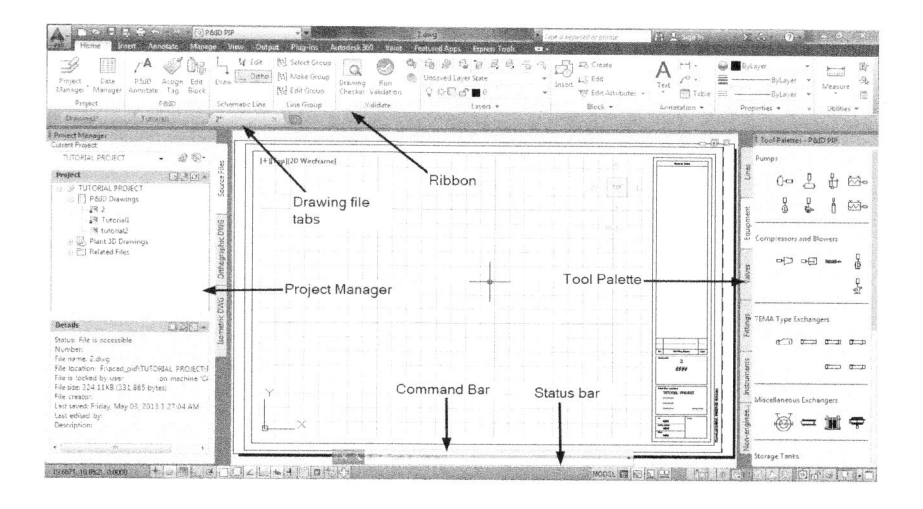

Tutorial 1

In this tutorial you will create your first P&ID.

Creating a New Project

- Start AutoCAD P&ID 2014.

- In the **PROJECT MANAGER**, select **New Project** from the drop-down; the **Project Setup Wizard** appears.

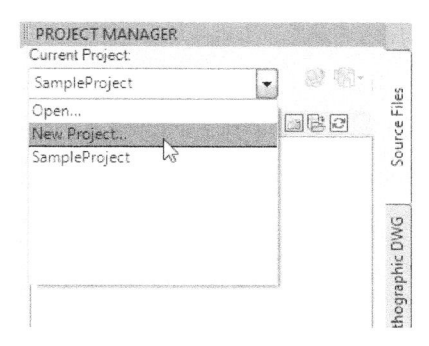

4

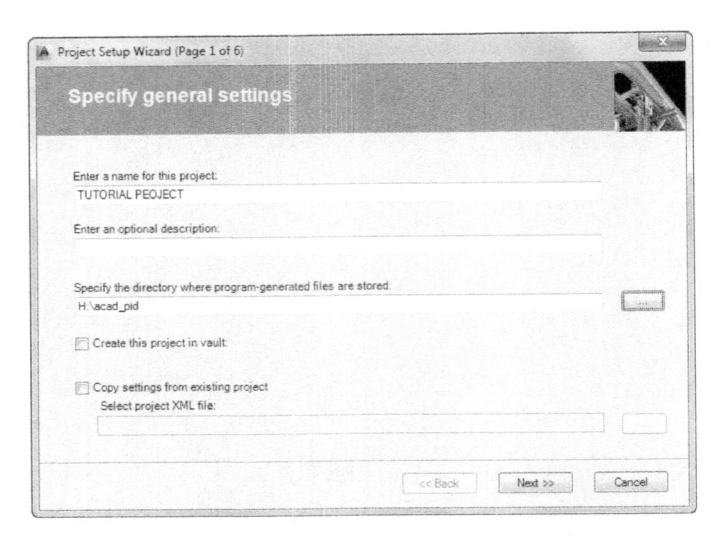

AutoCAD P&ID Tutorial

[Screenshot: Project Setup Wizard (Page 1 of 6) – Specify general settings, with "TUTORIAL PEOJECT" entered as the project name and "H:\acad_pid" as the directory.]

- Enter **TUTORIAL PROJECT** in the **Enter a name for this project** field.

- Specify the location of the program generated files and supporting files.

- Click the **Next** button; the **Specify unit settings** page appears

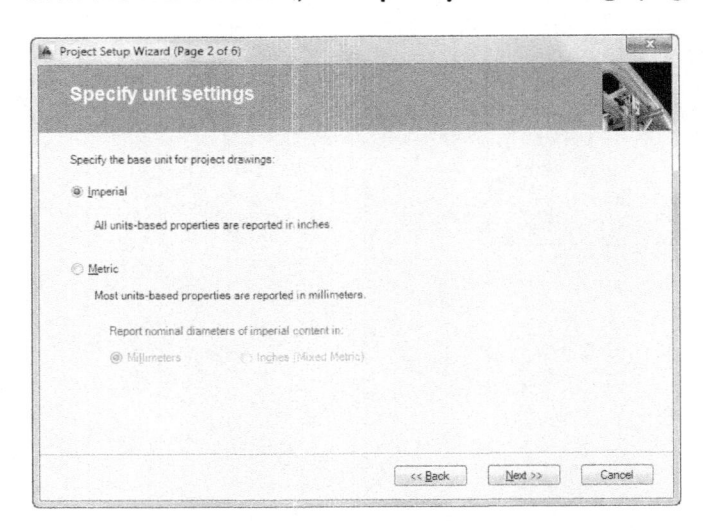

[Screenshot: Project Setup Wizard (Page 2 of 6) – Specify unit settings, with Imperial selected.]

- Select **Imperial** as the units for project drawings.

5

- Click the **Next** button; the **Specify P&ID settings** page appears.

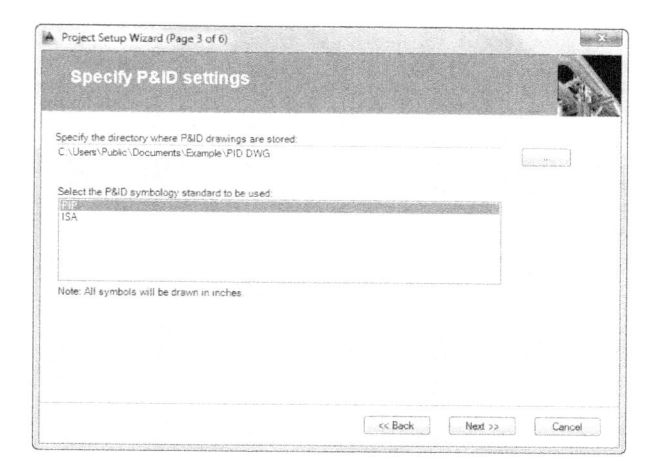

- Specify the directory where P&ID files will be saved.

- Select **PIP** as the P&ID symbology standard to be used.

- Click the **Next** button; the **Specify Plant 3D directory settings** page appears.

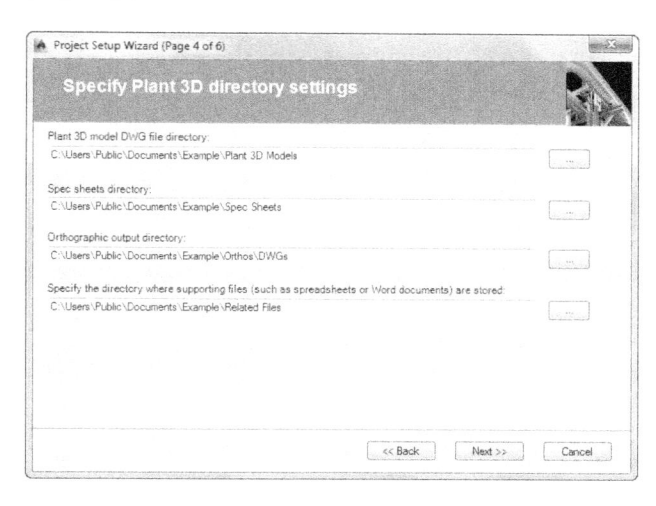

- Click the **Next** button; the **Specify database settings** page appears.

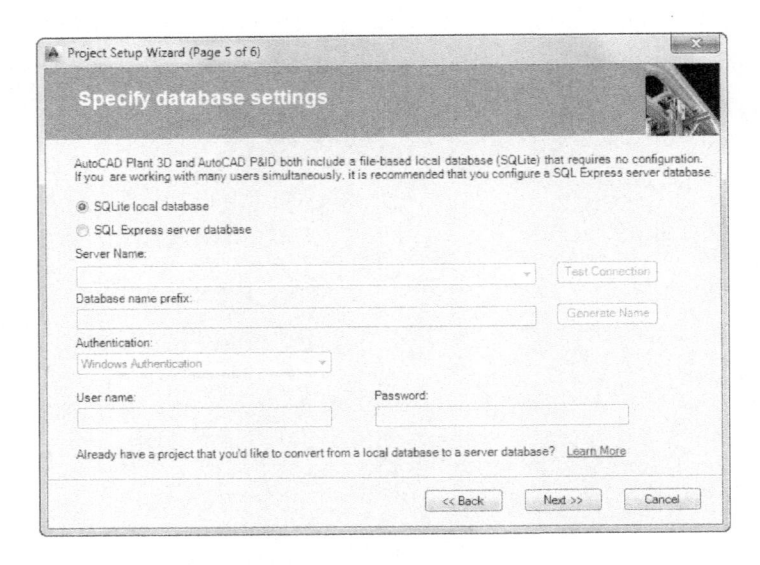

- Select the **SQLite local database** option if you are working on a standalone workstation.

- If you are working on a server, select the **SQL Express server database** option and configure the server settings.

- Click the **Next** button; the **Finish** page appears.

- Click **Finish** to create the new project.

Creating a New Drawing

- Right-click on **P&ID Drawings** and then choose **New Drawing**.

AutoCAD P&ID Tutorial

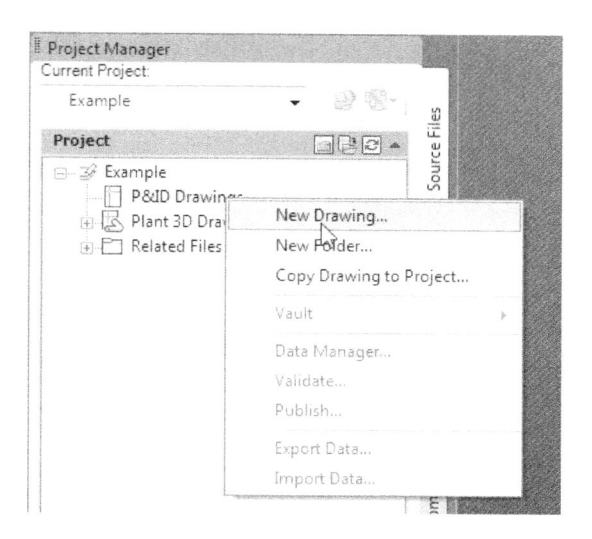

The **New DWG** dialog box appears.

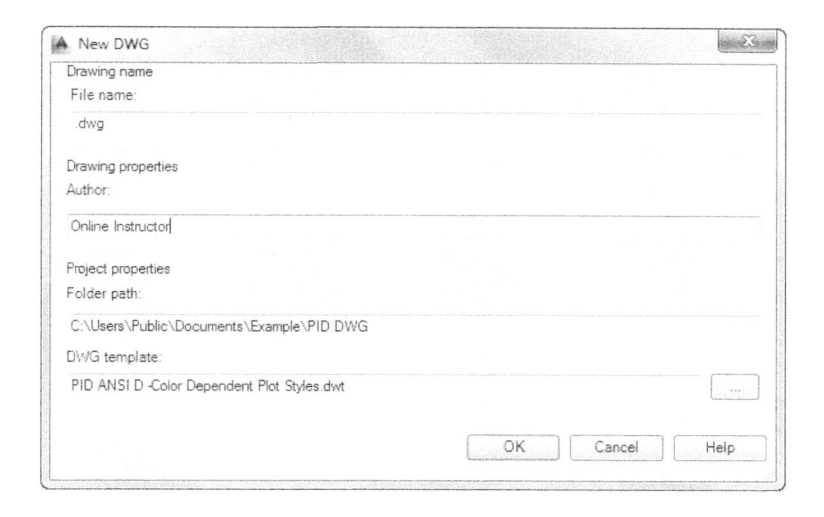

- Enter the file name in the **File name** field.

    The **PID ANSI D - Color Dependent Plot Styles.dwt** is the default template. You can select any other template by clicking the Browse button next to the **DWG template** field.

- Click **OK** to create a new P&ID file.

AutoCAD P&ID Tutorial

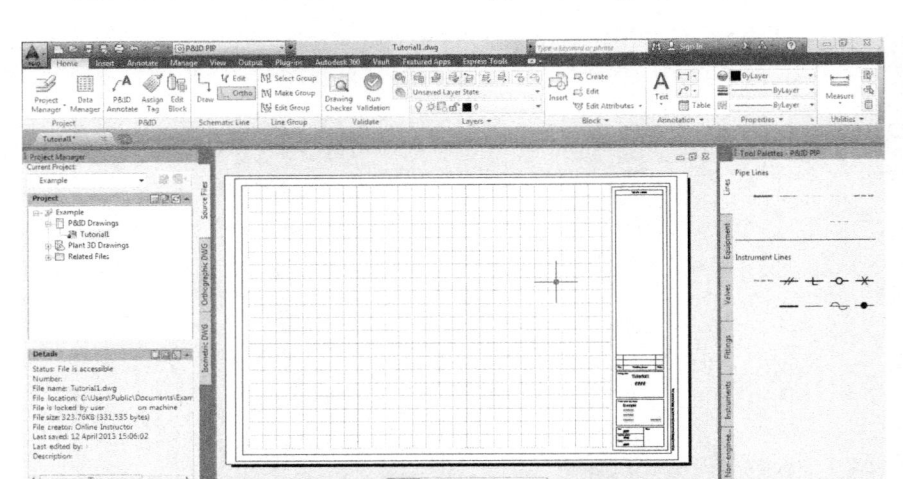

The default screen of P&ID file appears as given next.

You will notice that **Tool Palette** appears at the right-side of the screen. You can change the tools displayed on the **Tool Palette**. To do so, right-click on the title bar of the **Tool Palette**.

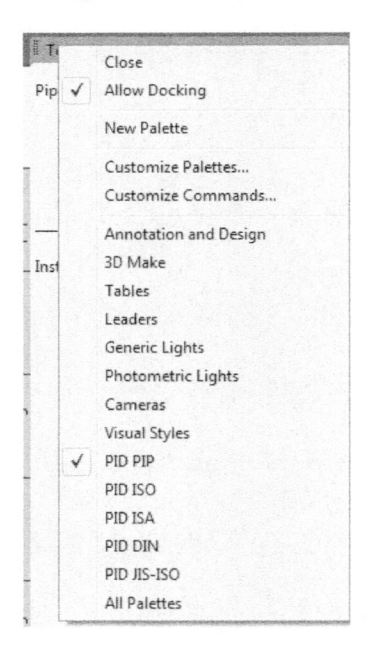

If the P&ID PIP tool palette is not displayed, click **P&ID PIP** on the shortcut menu to display the P&ID symbols of PIP standard.

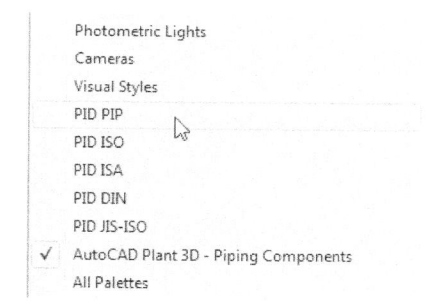

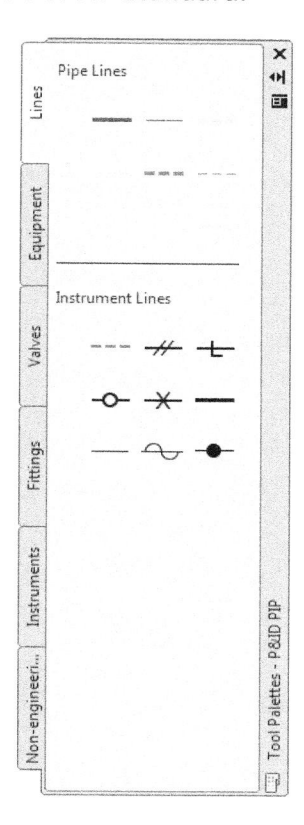

Viewing the Drawing Properties

- To view the drawing properties, right-click on the drawing file and select **Properties**; the **Drawing Properties** dialog box appears.

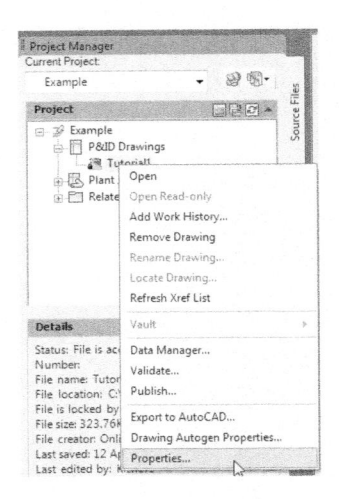

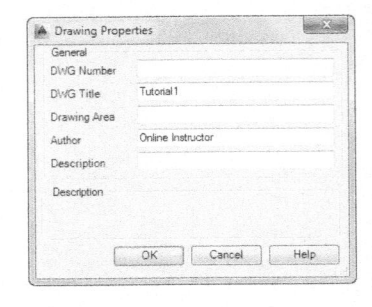

Placing Equipment

In this section, you will learn to place equipment. AutoCAD P&ID provides you with various pre-defined equipment. These equipments are located in the **Equipment** Tool Palette.

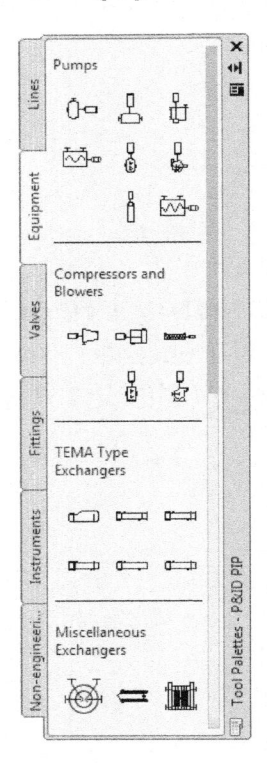

AutoCAD P&ID Tutorial

- On the Tool Palette, select the **Equipment** tab.

- Click the **Vessel** icon under **Vessels and Miscellaneous Vessel Details**.

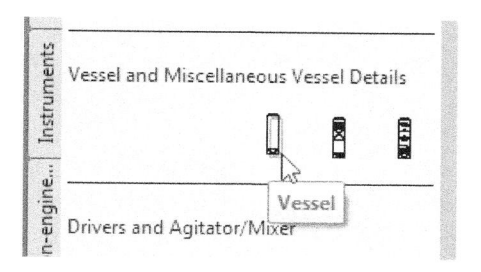

- To specify the location, click somewhere in the middle of the drawing area.

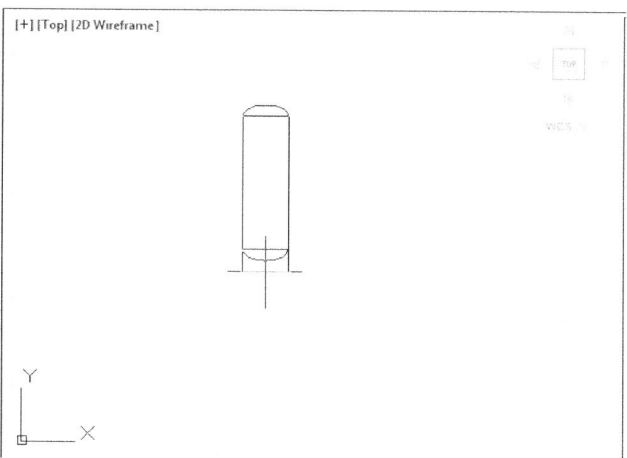

- Type 1.5 at the scale prompt and press **Enter** key to specify the scale factor.

  The **Assign Tag** dialog appears.

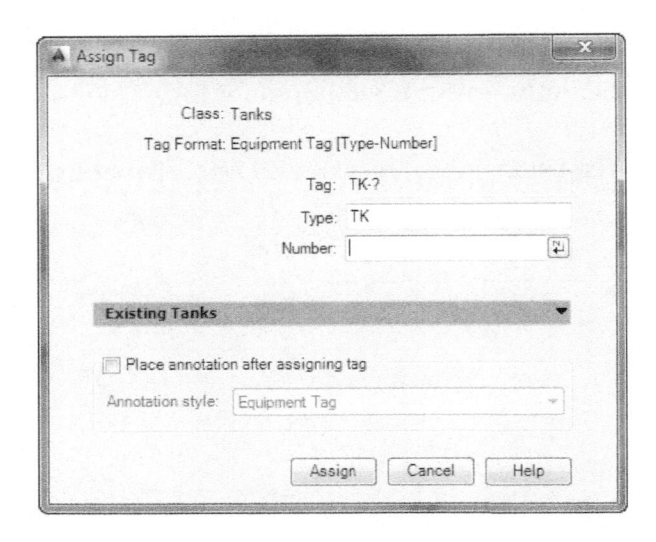

This dialog is used to add information to a P&ID component.

- To assign the tag, click the button next to the **Number** field.

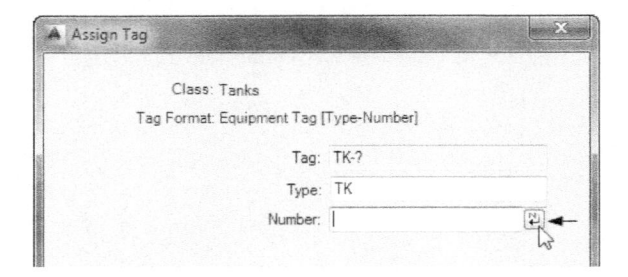

- Select the **Place annotation after assigning tag** option.

- Select **Equipment tag** as Annotation style.

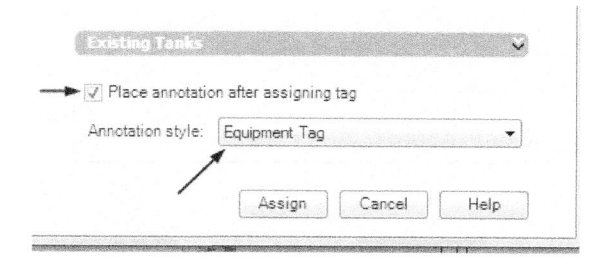

- Click **Assign** on the **Assign tag** dialog.
- Click above the vessel to place the annotation.

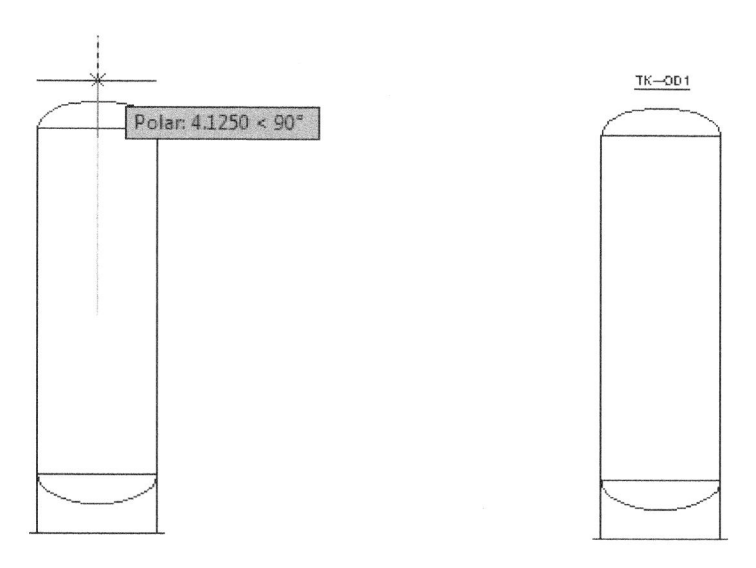

Next, place a Horizontal Centrifugal pump

- To place a pump, click the **Horizontal Centrifugal Pump** icon under the **Pumps** section.

AutoCAD P&ID Tutorial

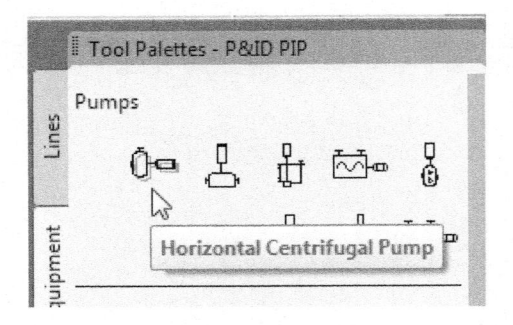

- Click somewhere near the bottom left of the vessel.

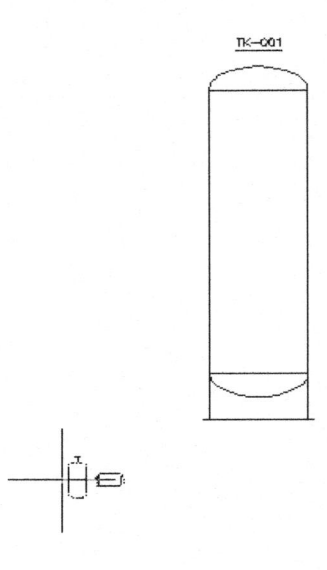

- To assign the tag, click the button next to the **Number** field.

- Click **Assign**.

- Place the tag below the pump.

AutoCAD P&ID Tutorial

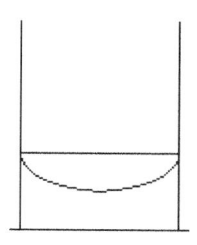

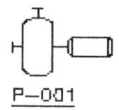

- Select the pump and its tag by dragging a window.

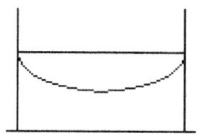

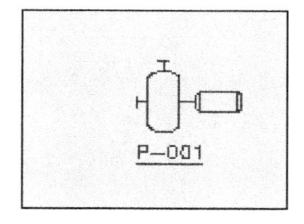

- Use the **COPY** command to copy the pump.

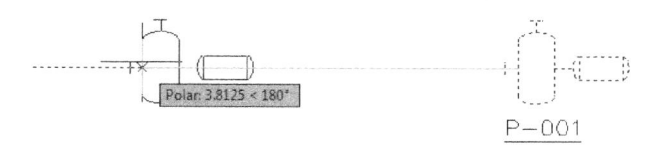

AutoCAD P&ID Tutorial

P-001?   P-001

Notice a question mark on the copied tag. To solve this, you have to update the tag.

- Right-click on the pump and choose **Assign Tag**.

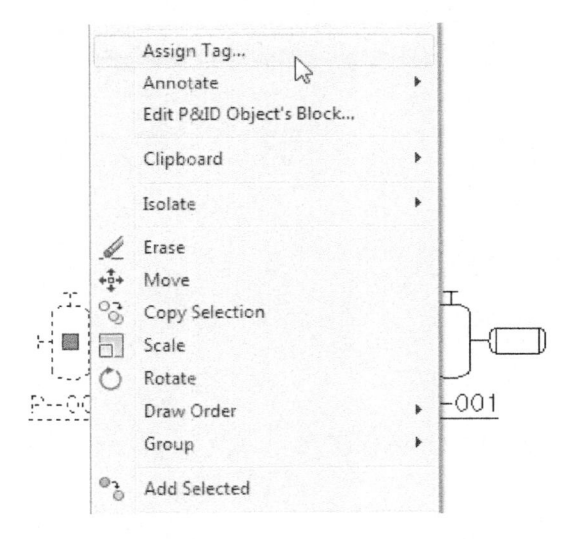

- Click the button next to the **Number** field and clear the **Place annotation after assigning tag** option.

- Click **Assign**.

AutoCAD P&ID Tutorial

P-002

P-001

- Similarly, place a TEMAtype BEM Exchanger on right side of the vessel.

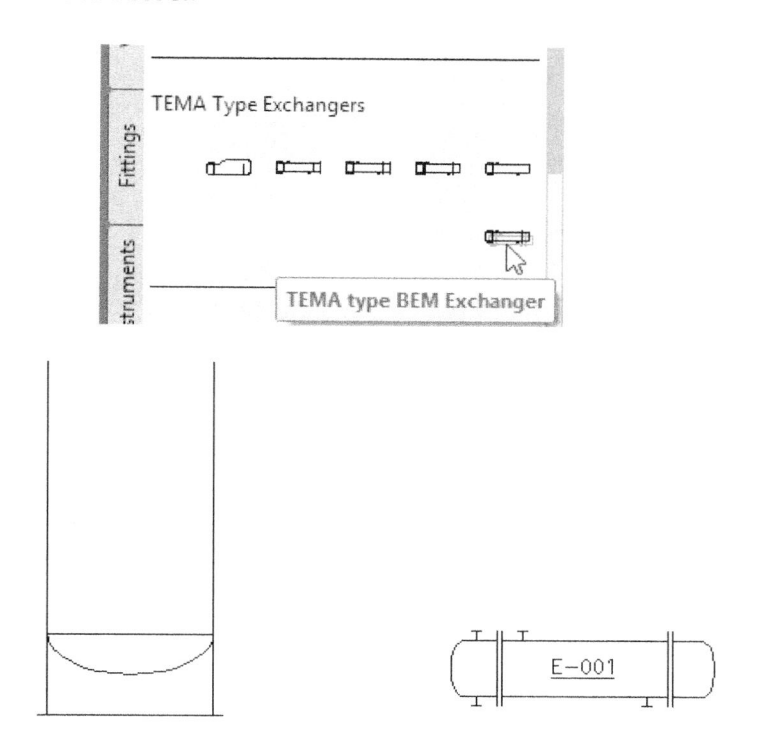

E-001

The P&ID after placing all the vessels looks as shown below.

AutoCAD P&ID Tutorial

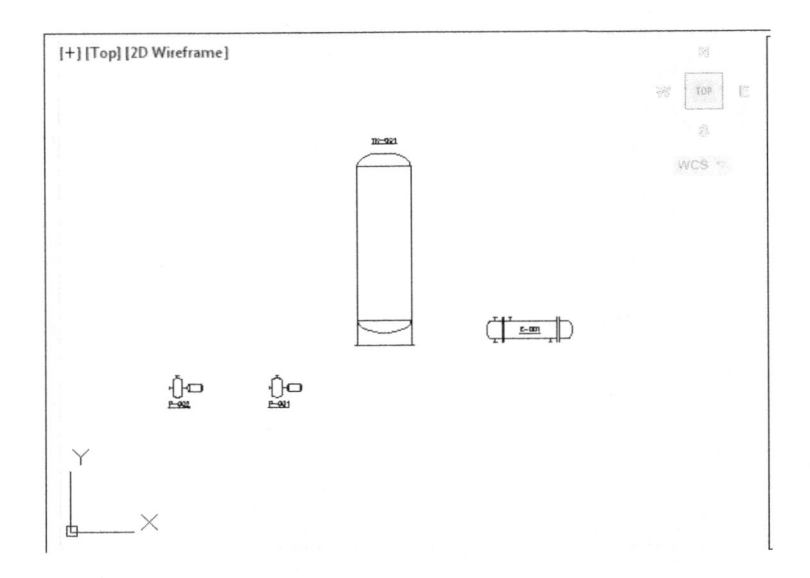

Editing the P&ID Symbols

During the design process, you may require to edit the exiting P&ID symbols. In this example, you will modify the vertical vessel.

- To edit the vertical vessel, right-click on it and choose **Edit P&ID Object's Block.**

AutoCAD P&ID Tutorial

The AutoCAD Block editor appears.

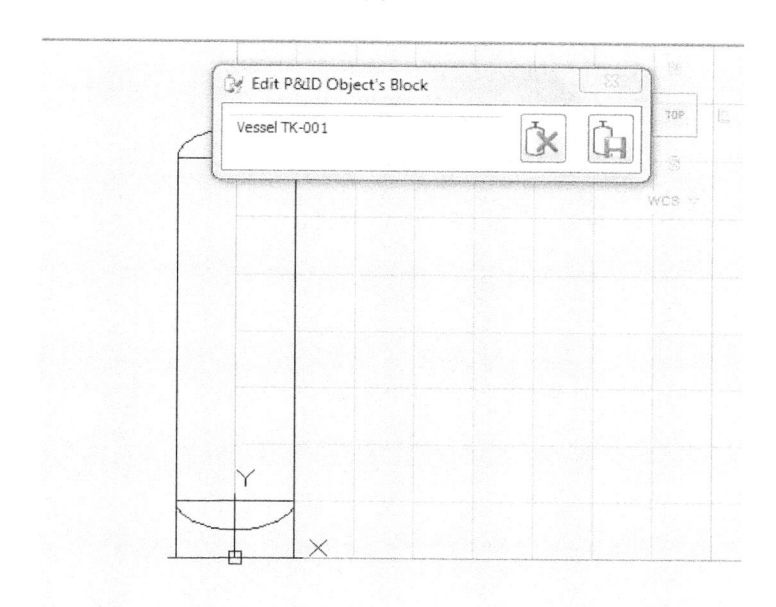

- Modify the Vessel block.

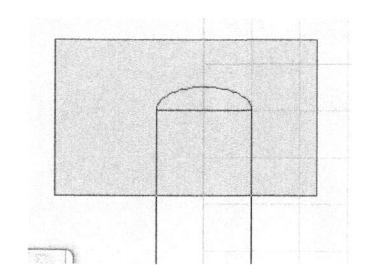

AutoCAD P&ID Tutorial

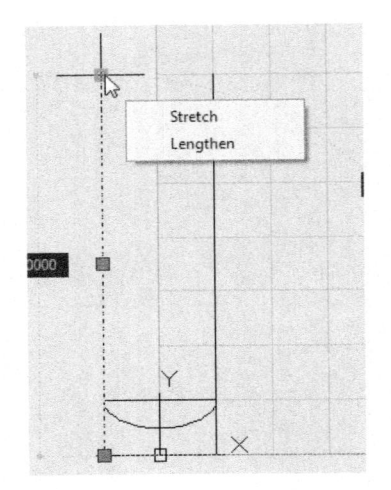

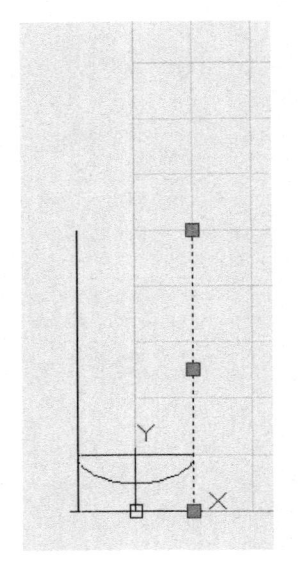

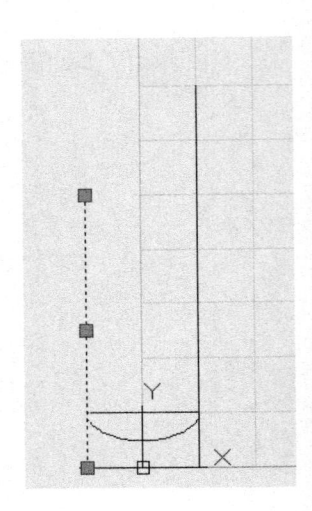

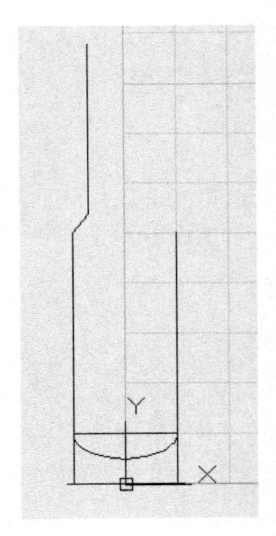

AutoCAD P&ID Tutorial

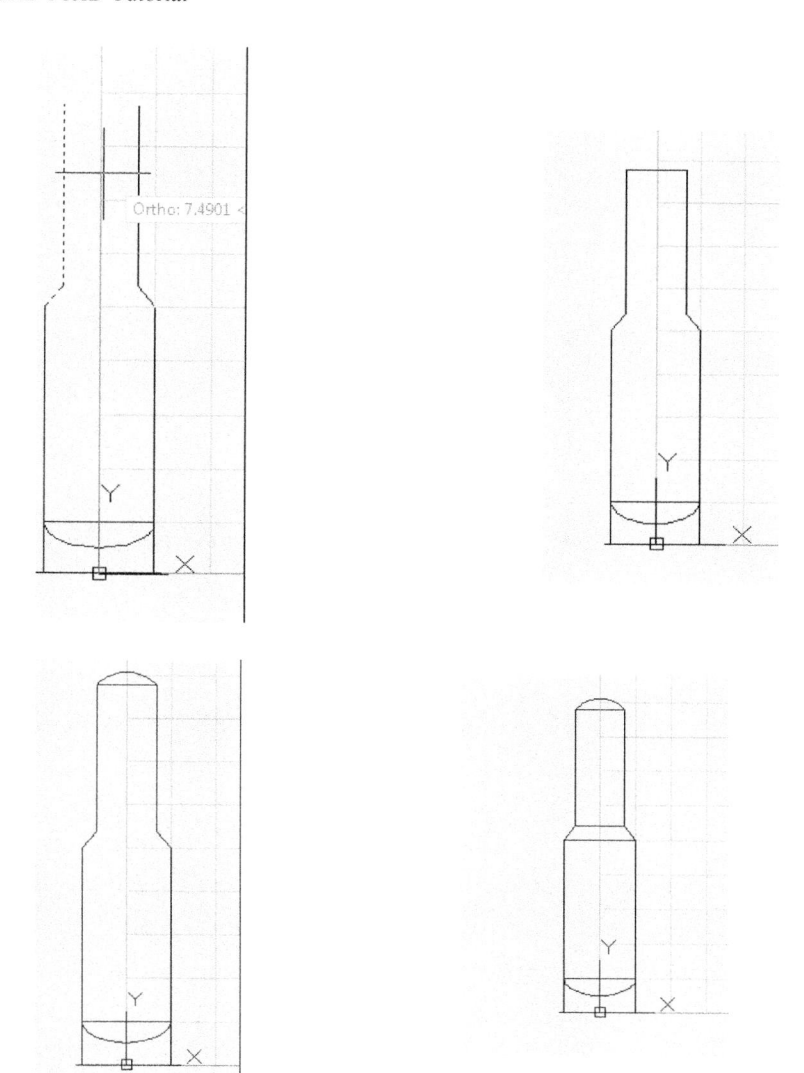

- Click the **Save** button

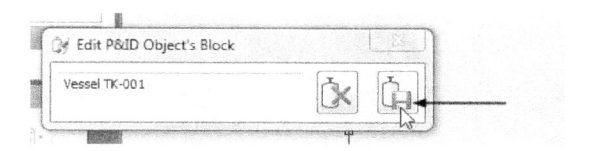

The P&ID symbol after editing.

TK-001

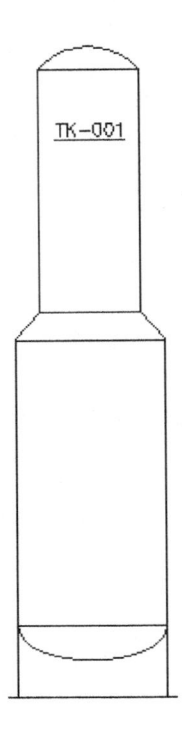

Adding Nozzles to the Equipment

Nozzles are required to connect equipment with a pipe. Most of the nozzles are automatically added when you connect an equipment with a pipe. Sometimes, you may need to manually add nozzles to equipment.

- To add nozzles to equipment, click the **Fittings** tab on the Tool Palette.

AutoCAD P&ID Tutorial

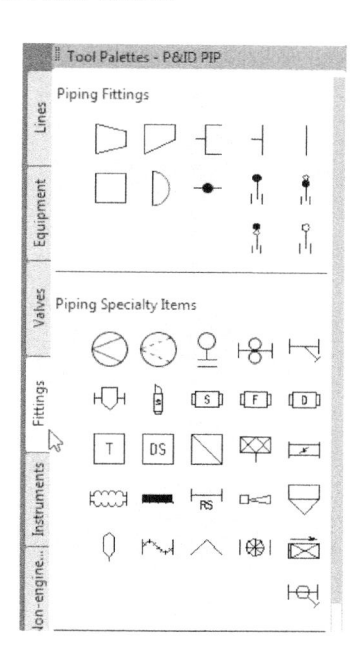

- Click the **Single Line Nozzle** icon under the **Nozzles** section.

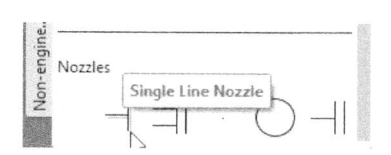

- Select the vertical vessel from the drawing.

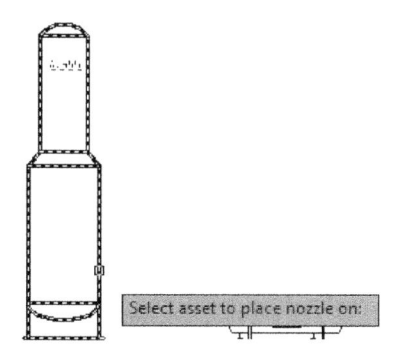

- Specify the insertion point as shown in figure.

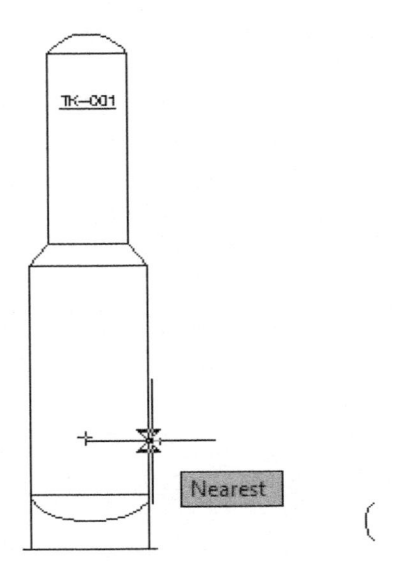

- Enter 0 as the angle of rotation.

- Similarly, place another nozzle on the vessel.

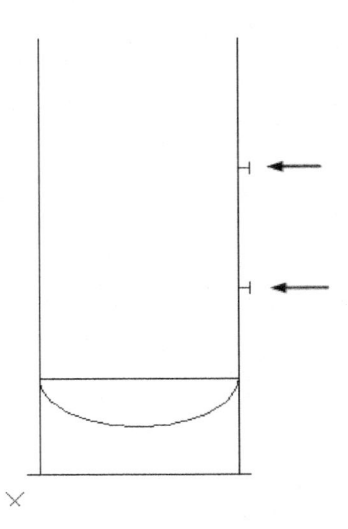

- To add annotation, right-click on the nozzle and choose **Annotation > Tag**.

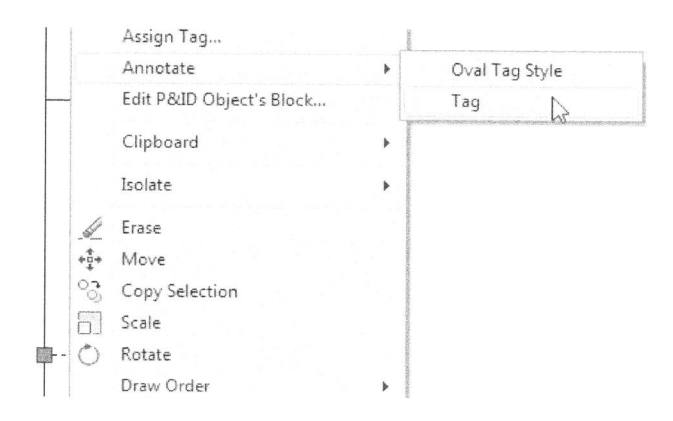

Creating Pipe Lines

Pipe lines are the important part of a P&ID. They circulate the needed fluids or gasses within a plant. In AutoCAD P&ID, you can create pipe lines using the tools available in the **Lines** tool palette.

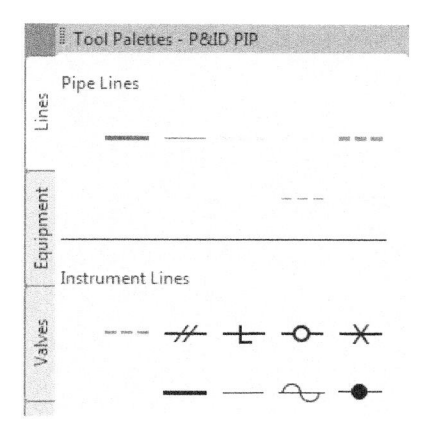

- To create a pipe line, click the **Primary Line Segment** icon under the **Pipe Lines** section.

AutoCAD P&ID Tutorial

[Tool Palettes - P&ID PIP showing Pipe Lines > Primary Line Segment]

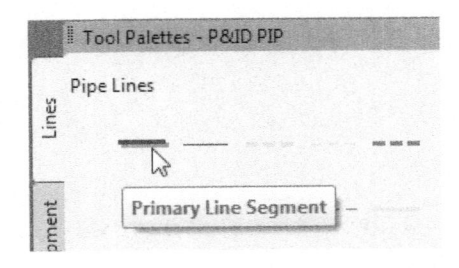

- Click on the top portion of the vertical vessel.

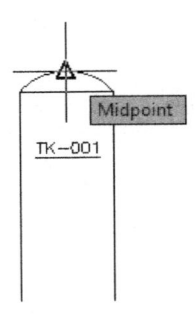

[Image: TK-001 vessel with Midpoint snap indicated on top]

- Move the cursor upward and click.

- Move the cursor right-ward and click.

- Press **Enter** key.

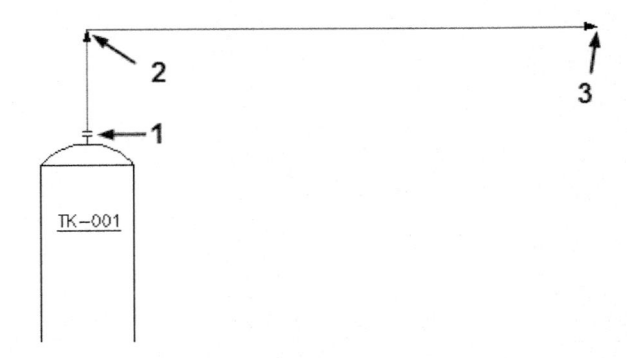

[Image: TK-001 vessel with nozzle and pipe line, points labeled 1, 2, 3]

You will notice that the nozzle is created automatically.

AutoCAD P&ID Tutorial

- To create a pipe line between the vertical vessel and pump, click the **Primary Line Segment** icon and select the nozzle of the pump as shown in figure.

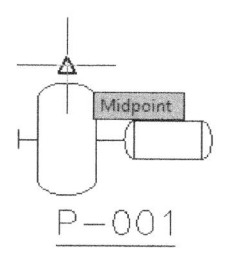

- Move the cursor upward and click.

- Move the cursor right-ward and click on the vessel.

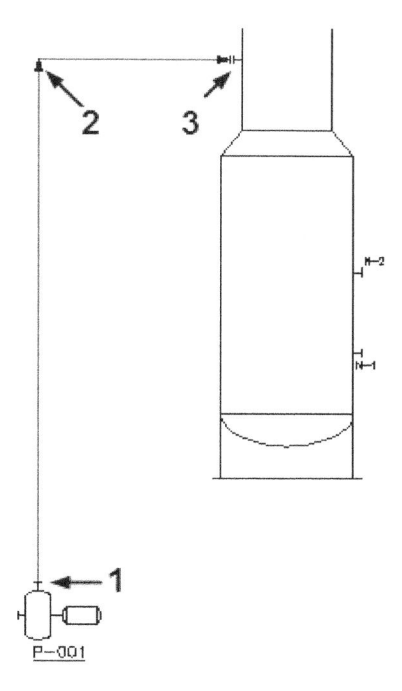

- Similarly, create a line between the two pumps

AutoCAD P&ID Tutorial

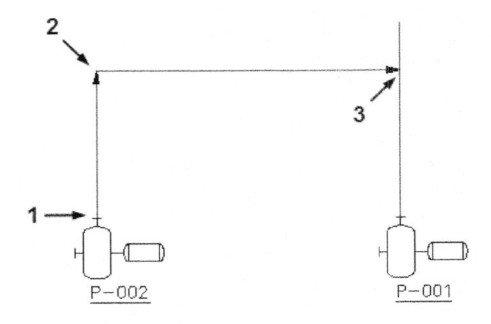

- Create an inlet pipe line connecting the pump.

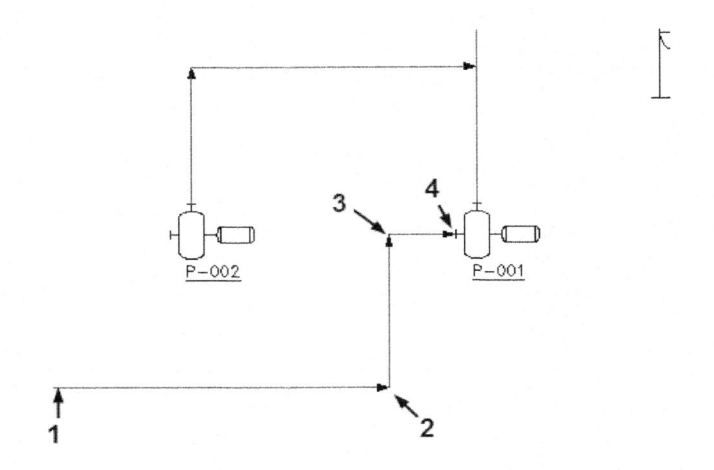

- Create an inlet pipe to another pump.

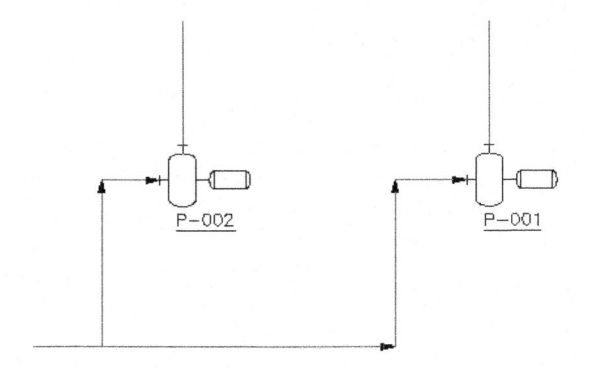

AutoCAD P&ID Tutorial

- Create the other pipe lines in the P&ID.

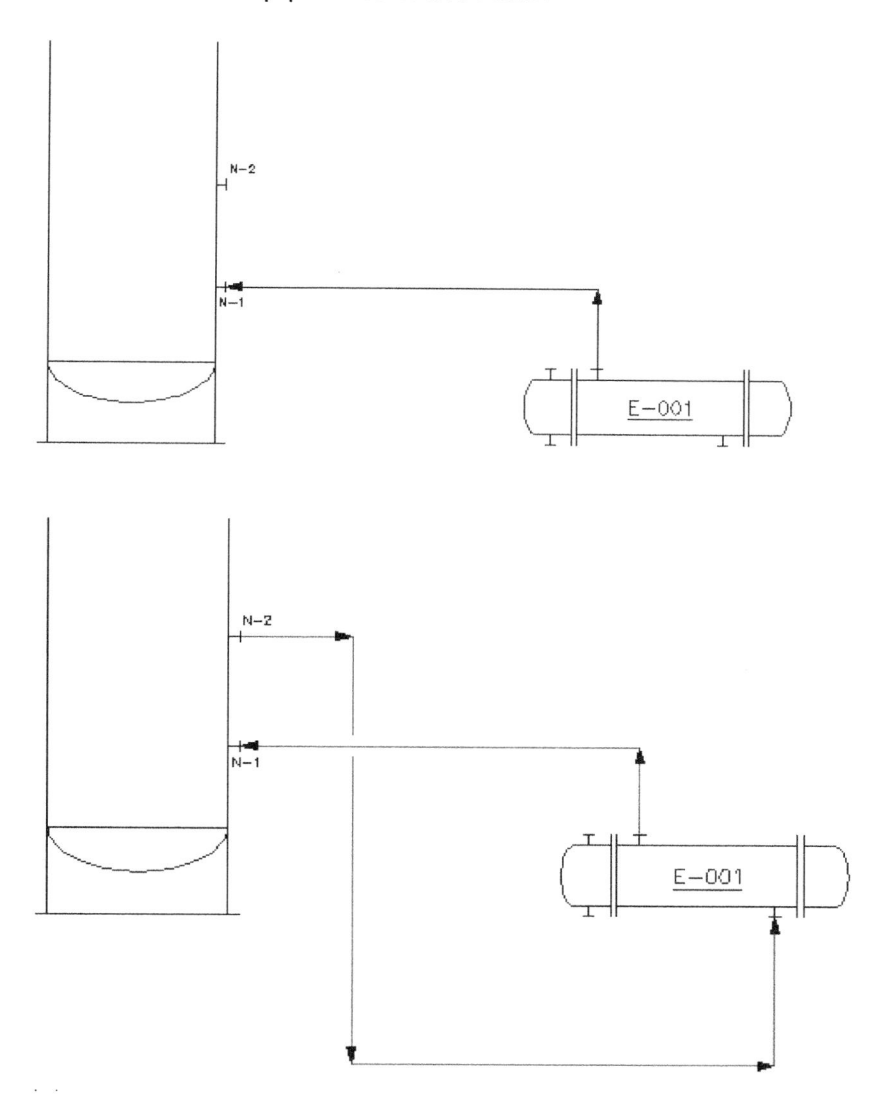

AutoCAD P&ID Tutorial

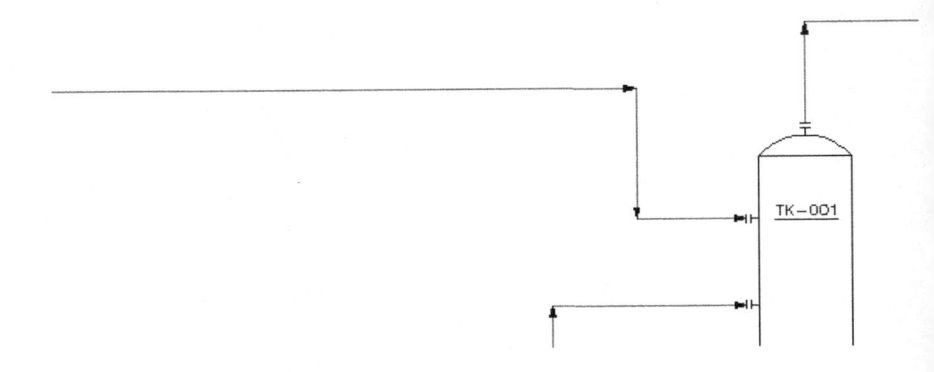

The P&ID after adding all the lines is shown in figure below.

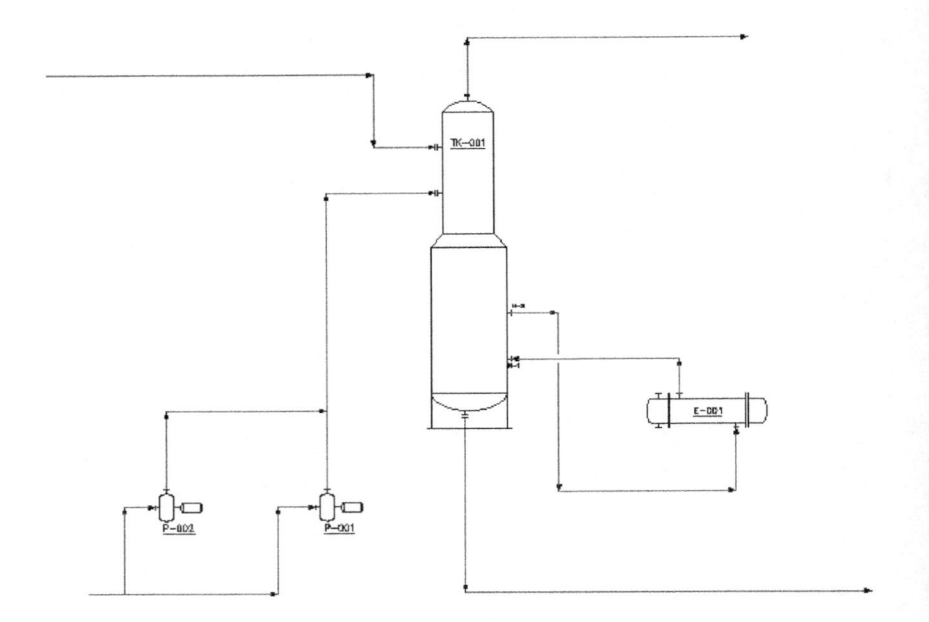

Assigning Tags to lines

In a P&ID, the lines represent the pipes in the real plant. You have to show the information related to the pipe lines by assigning tags.

AutoCAD P&ID Tutorial

- To assign tag to a line, click the **Assign Tag** button on the **P&ID** panel of the **Home** ribbon.

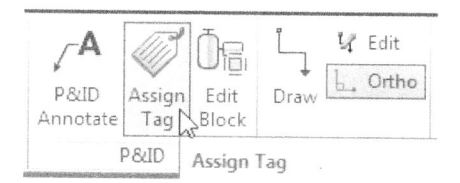

- Select the inlet line of the pumps.

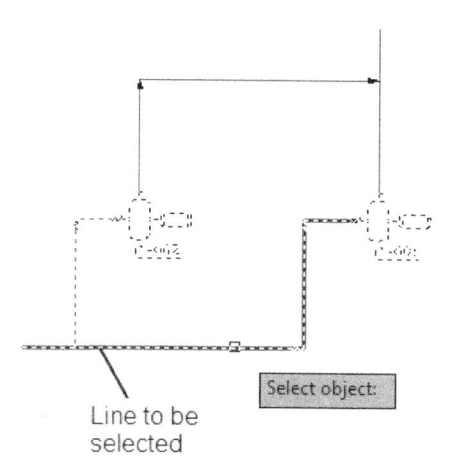

Line to be selected

- Press Enter key.

The **Assign Tag** dialog appears.

- Enter the following information in this dialog.

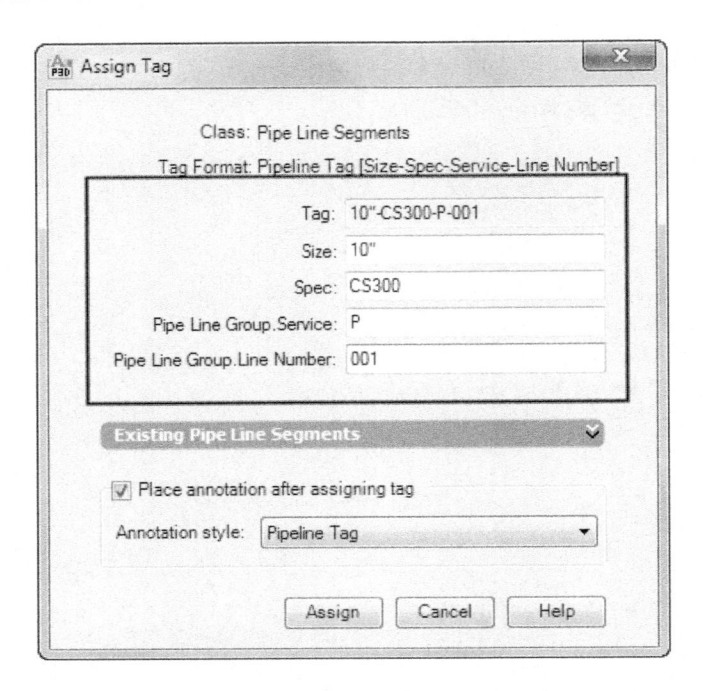

- Select the **Place annotation after assigning tag** option and click **Assign**.

- Place the annotation below the line.

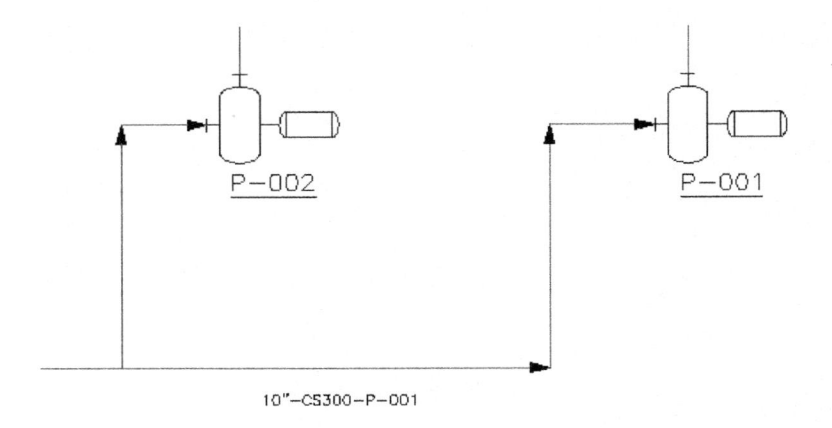

Next, you have to group two lines and assign a tag to them.

AutoCAD P&ID Tutorial

- To group lines, click the **Make Group** button on the **Line Group** panel of the **Home** ribbon.

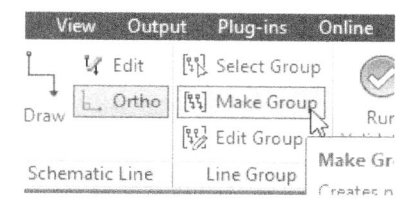

- Select the lines connecting the vessel and the pumps.

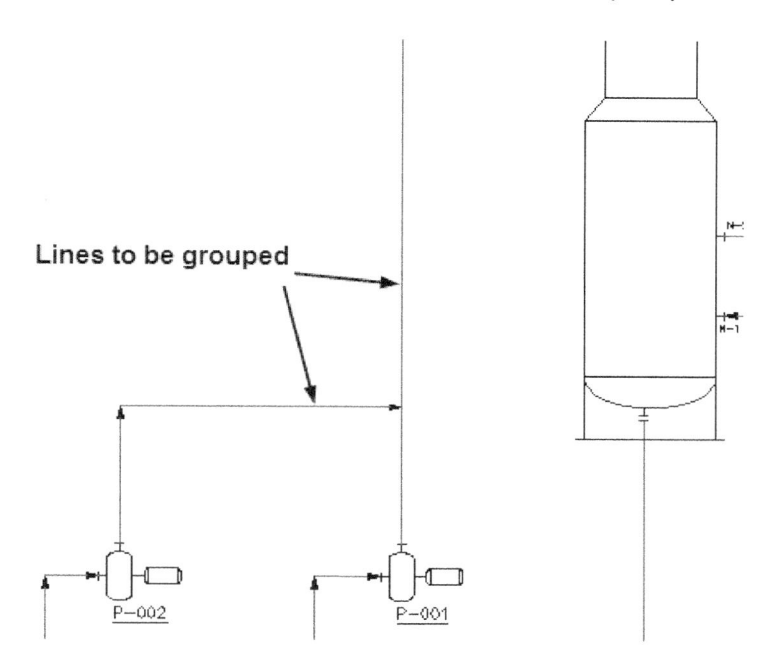

- Press **Enter** key to group the lines.

- Right-click on the line connecting the pumps and the vertical vessel.

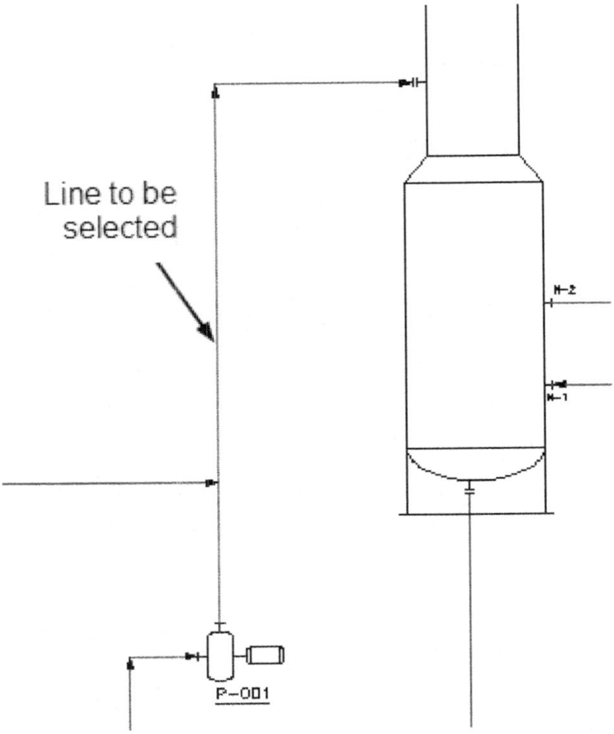
Line to be
selected
P-001

- Choose **Assign Tag** from the shortcut menu.
- Enter the information in the **Assign Tag** dialog.

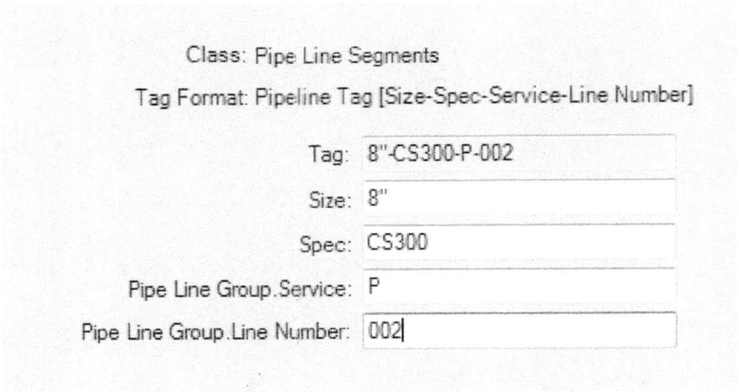
Class: Pipe Line Segments
Tag Format: Pipeline Tag [Size-Spec-Service-Line Number]
Tag: 8"-CS300-P-002
Size: 8"
Spec: CS300
Pipe Line Group.Service: P
Pipe Line Group.Line Number: 002

- Place the annotation next to the line.

AutoCAD P&ID Tutorial

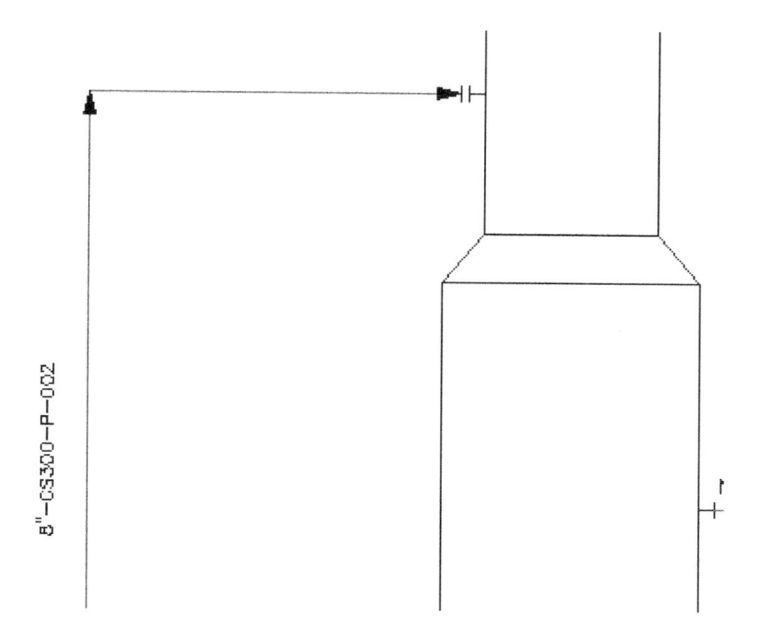

- Hover the cursor on the pipe connecting the second pump. The information related to the pipe is displayed.

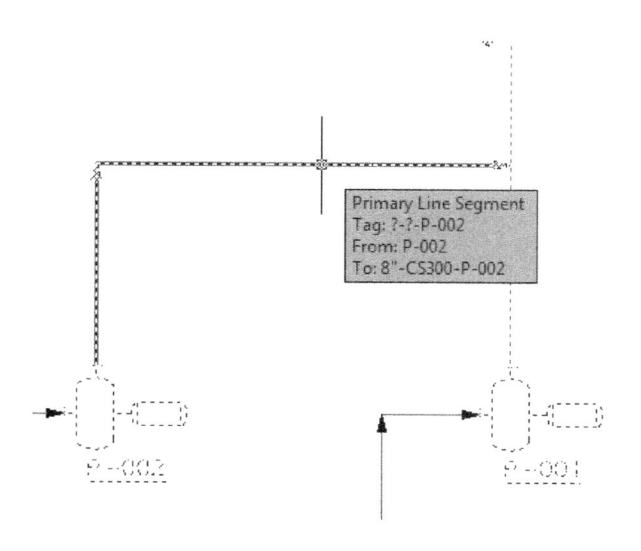

You will notice that the tag information is partially applied to the line. You have to specify the line size and spec of the pipe line.

AutoCAD P&ID Tutorial

- Right-click on the line and choose **Assign Tag** from the shortcut menu.

- Enter the **Size** and **Spec** in the **Assign Tag** dialog.

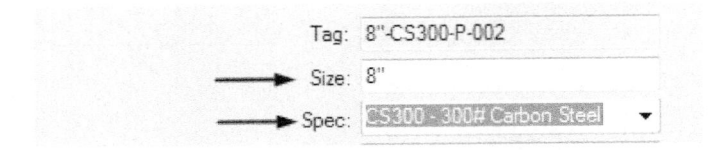

    Tag: 8"-CS300-P-002
    ⟶ Size: 8"
    ⟶ Spec: CS300 - 300# Carbon Steel

- Click **Assign**.

- Place the tag above the line.

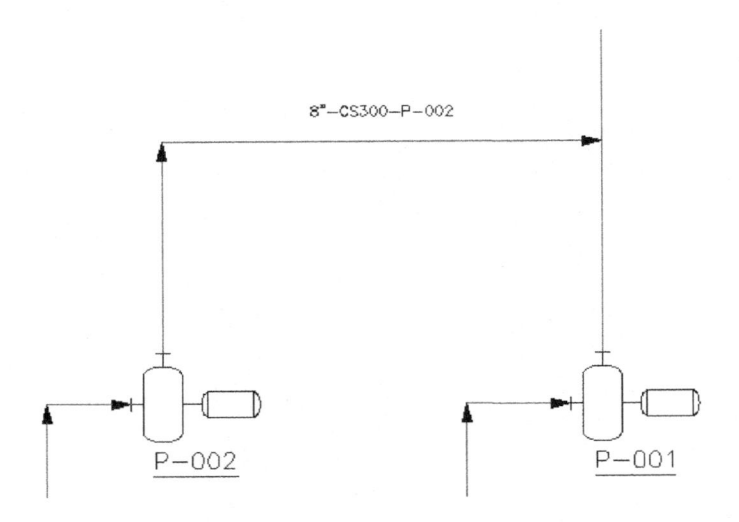

- Similarly, add tag information to other lines in the P&ID.

AutoCAD P&ID Tutorial

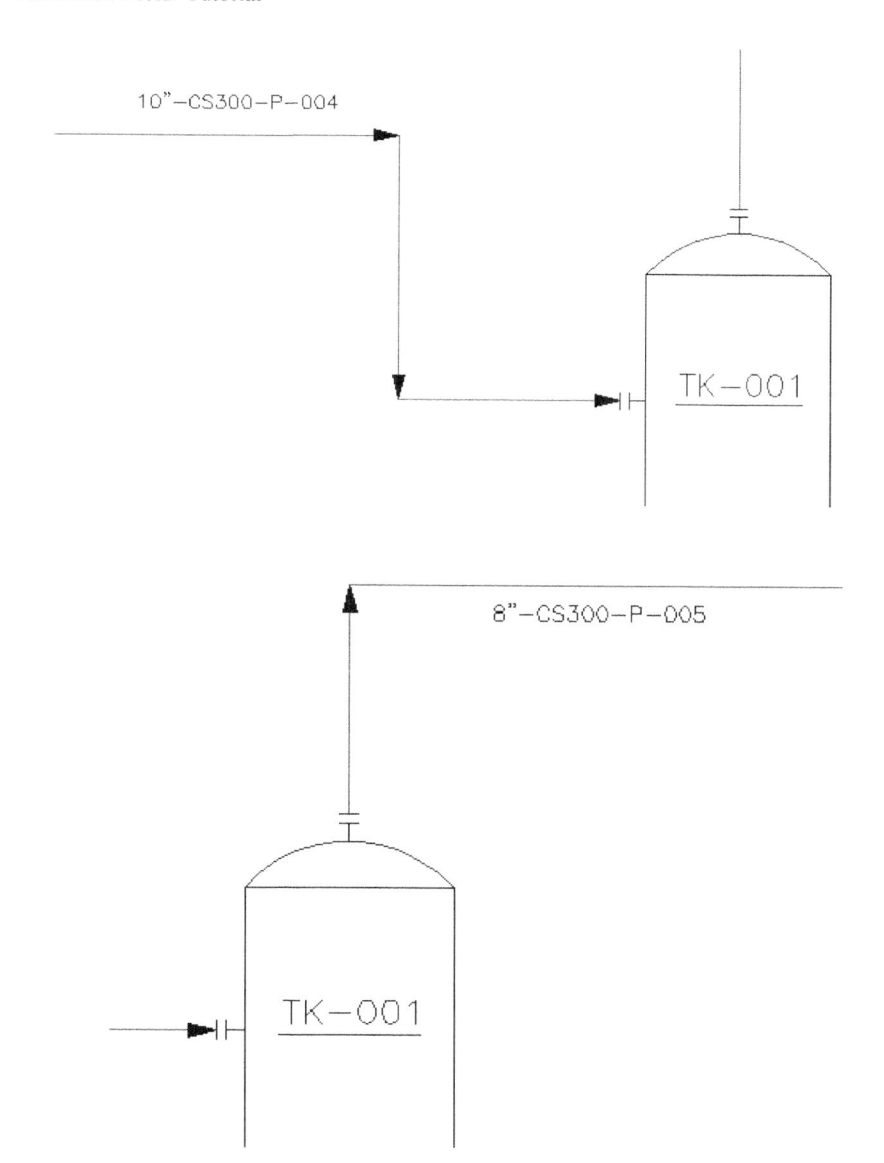

10"-CS300-P-004

TK-001

8"-CS300-P-005

TK-001

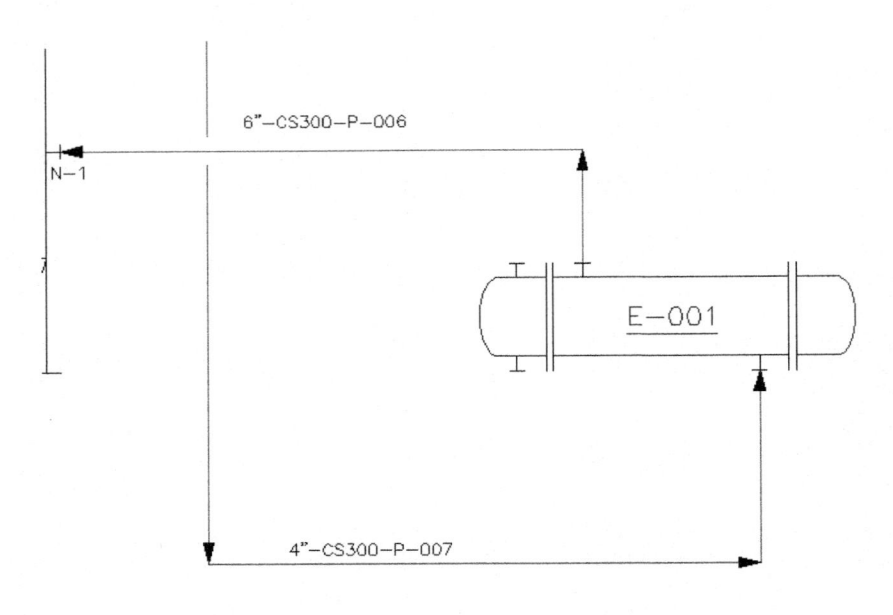

AutoCAD P&ID Tutorial

6"-CS300-P-006

N-1

E-001

4"-CS300-P-007

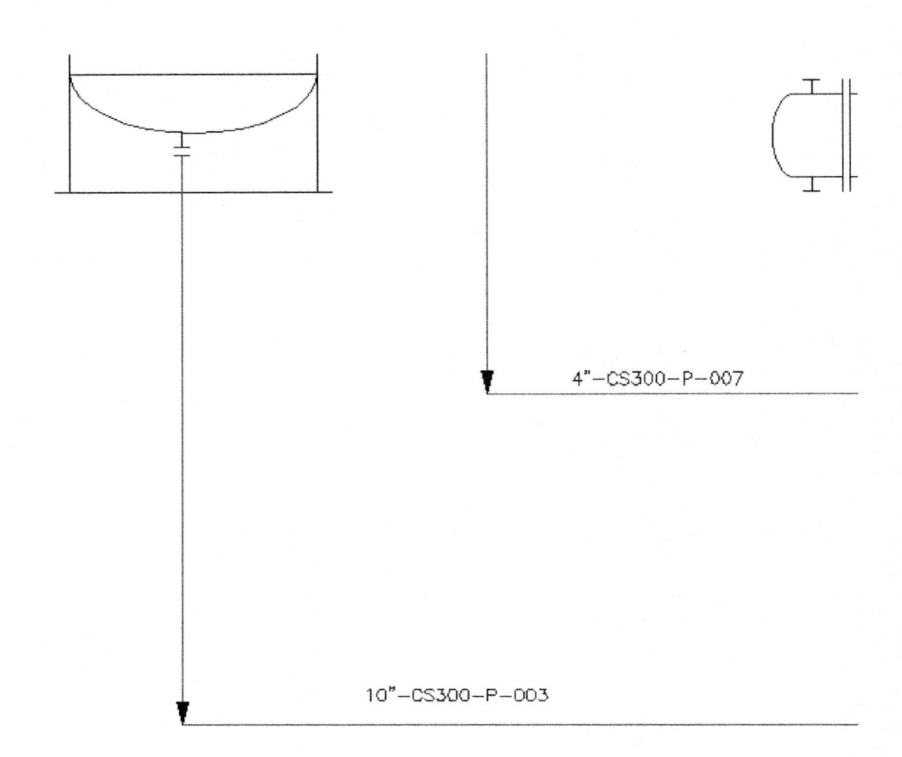

4"-CS300-P-007

10"-CS300-P-003

Placing Valves and Fittings

Valves and fittings are important part of a P&ID. They control the flow and flow direction of the fluid. You can find valve and fitting symbols on the **Valves** tab and **Fittings** tab, respectively.

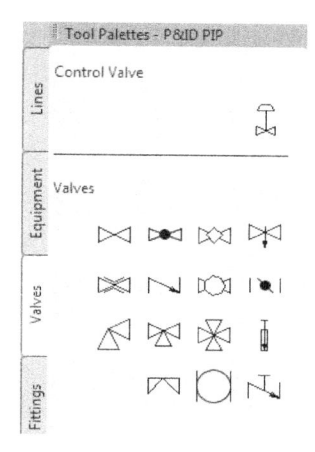

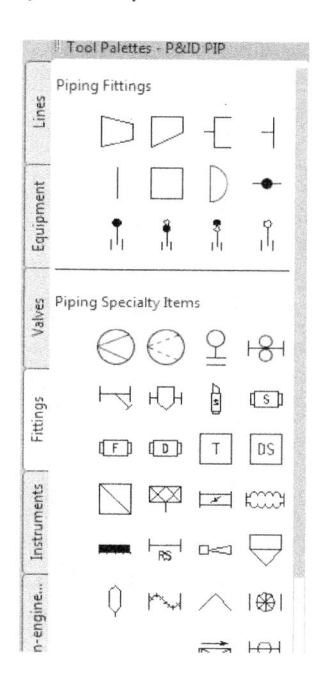

- To place a check valve, click the **Check Valve** icon on the **Valves** tool palette.

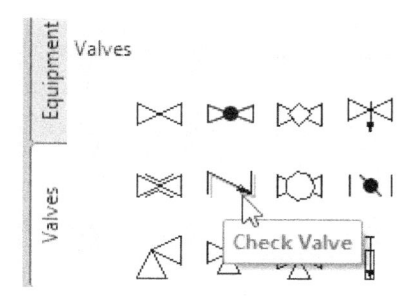

- Place on the line connecting the pump.

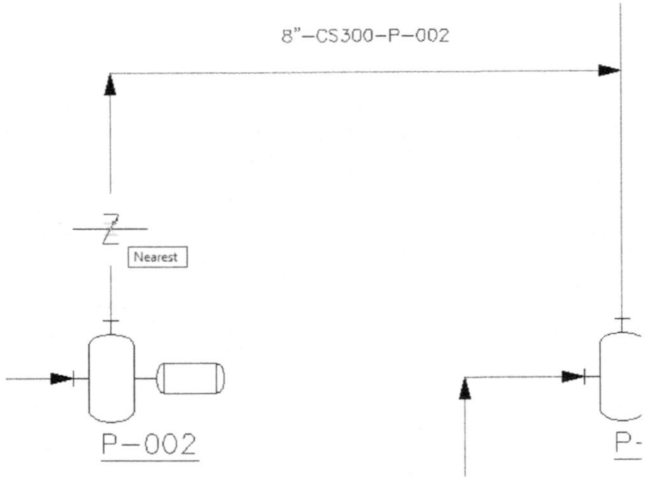
8"–CS300–P–002
Nearest
P–002
P-

- Place another check valve.

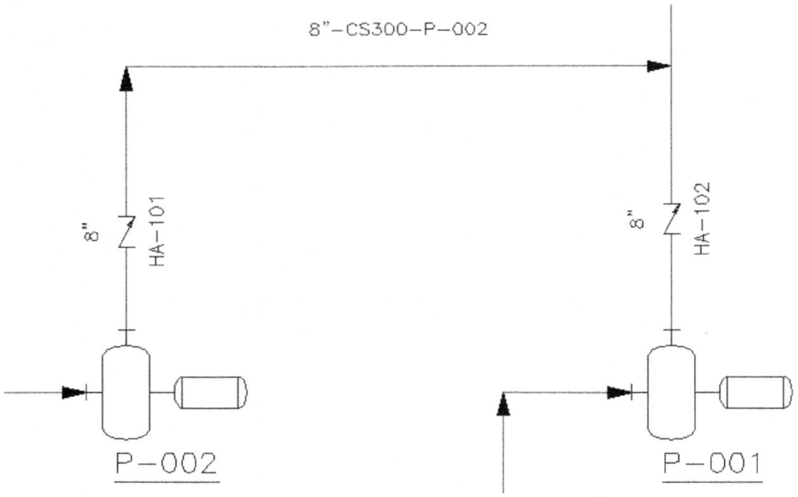
8"–CS300–P–002
8"
HA–101
8"
HA–102
P–002
P–001

Now, you have to place reducers.

- To place a reducer, click the **Fittings** tab on the Tool Palettes.
- Click the **Concentric Reducer** icon under the **Pipe Fittings** section.

AutoCAD P&ID Tutorial

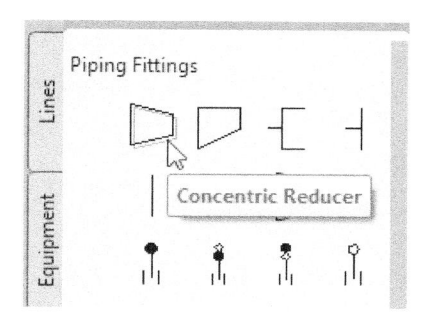

- Place on the line connecting the bottom of the vessel.

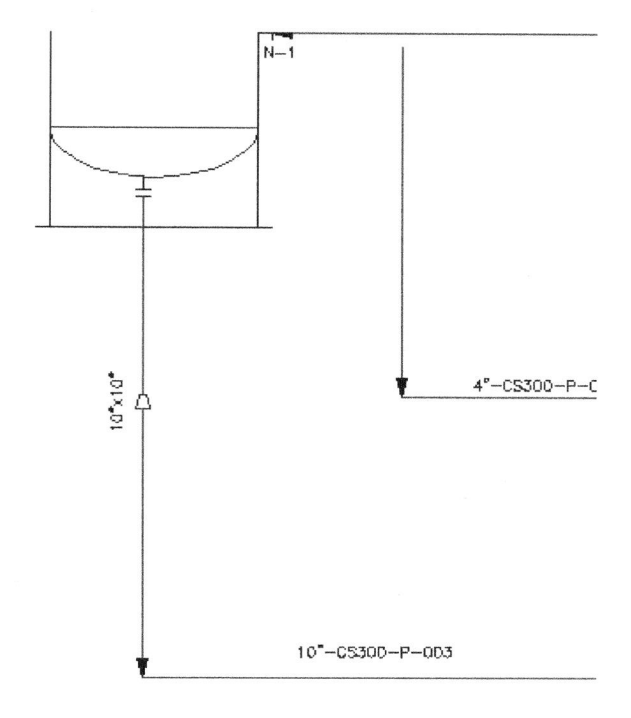

- Click the **Assign Tag** button on the **P&ID** panel of the **Home** ribbon.

- Select the line segment below the reducer.

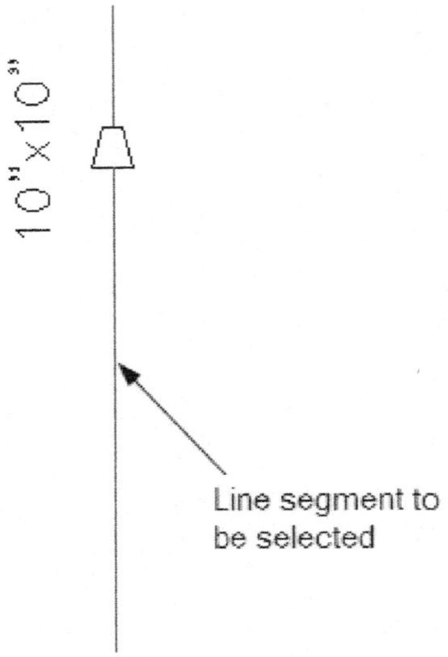
10"x10"
Line segment to
be selected

- Press **Enter** key.
- In the **Assign Tag** dialog, change the **Size** to 8".

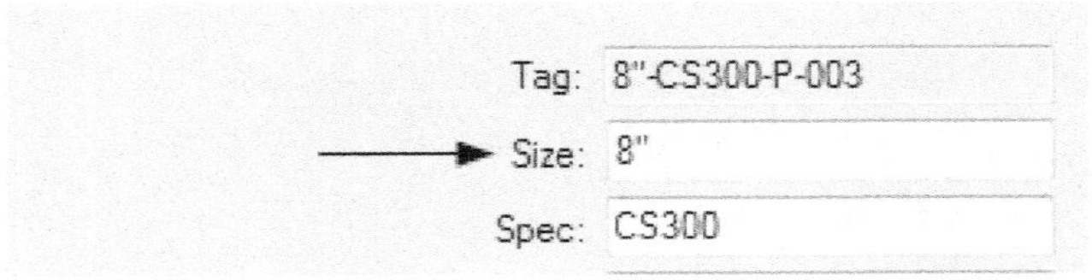
Tag: 8"-CS300-P-003
Size: 8"
Spec: CS300

- Clear the **Place annotation after assigning tag** option
- Click **Assign**.

The orientation of the reducer will change.

AutoCAD P&ID Tutorial

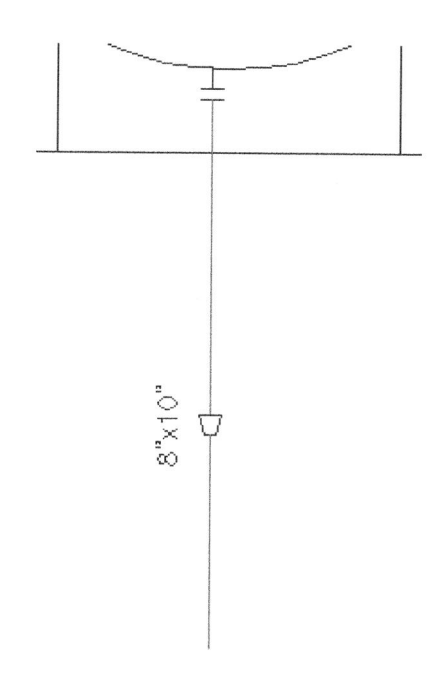

- Place another concentric reducer at the location shown below

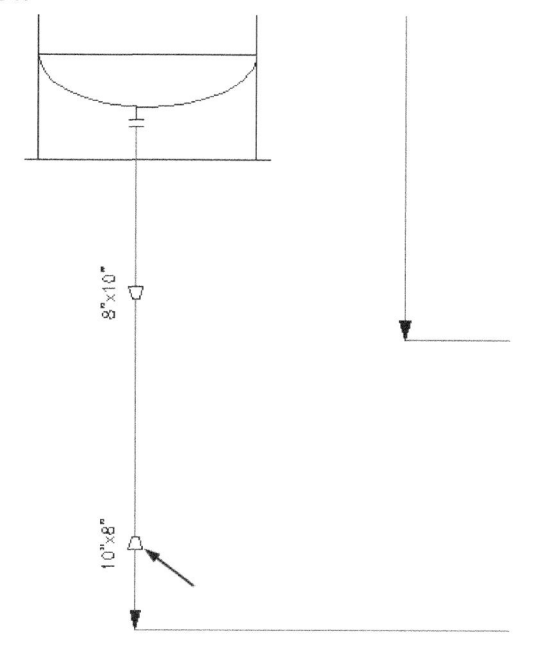

AutoCAD P&ID Tutorial

Next, you have to place a gate valve.

- To place a gate valve, click the **Gate Valve** icon on the **Valves** tool palette.

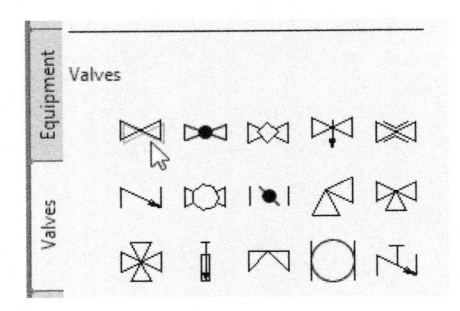

- Place it at the location shown in figure.

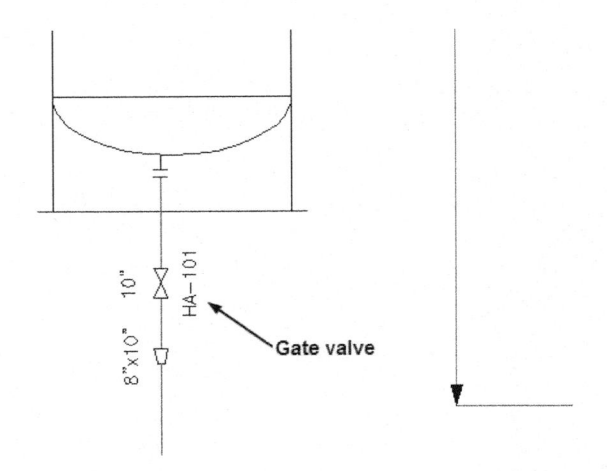

Gate valve

Similarly, place valves on lines connecting the pumps.

AutoCAD P&ID Tutorial

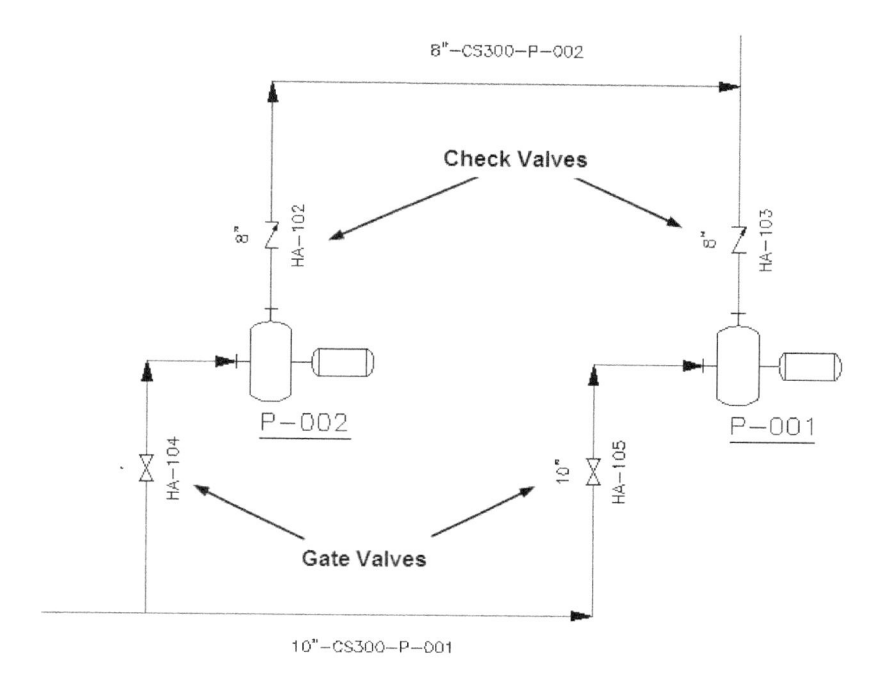

[Diagram showing piping layout with check valves (HA-102, HA-103) at top connected by pipe 8"-CS300-P-002, vessels P-002 and P-001, gate valves (HA-104, HA-105) at bottom connected by pipe 10"-CS300-P-001]

Placing Instruments

In a P&ID, the instrumentation which controls the operation of the plant equipment is represented by the instrument symbols. These symbols are located in the **Instruments** tool palette. This tool palette is divided into many sections based on the use of the instrument symbols.

The **Control Valve** section contains the flow control valve symbol.

The **Relief Valve** section contains the symbols of various pressure relief valves.

The **Primary Element Symbols (Flow)** section contains the symbols related to flow measuring instruments.

AutoCAD P&ID Tutorial

The **General Instruments** section contains the instrument symbols related to the process control instruments.

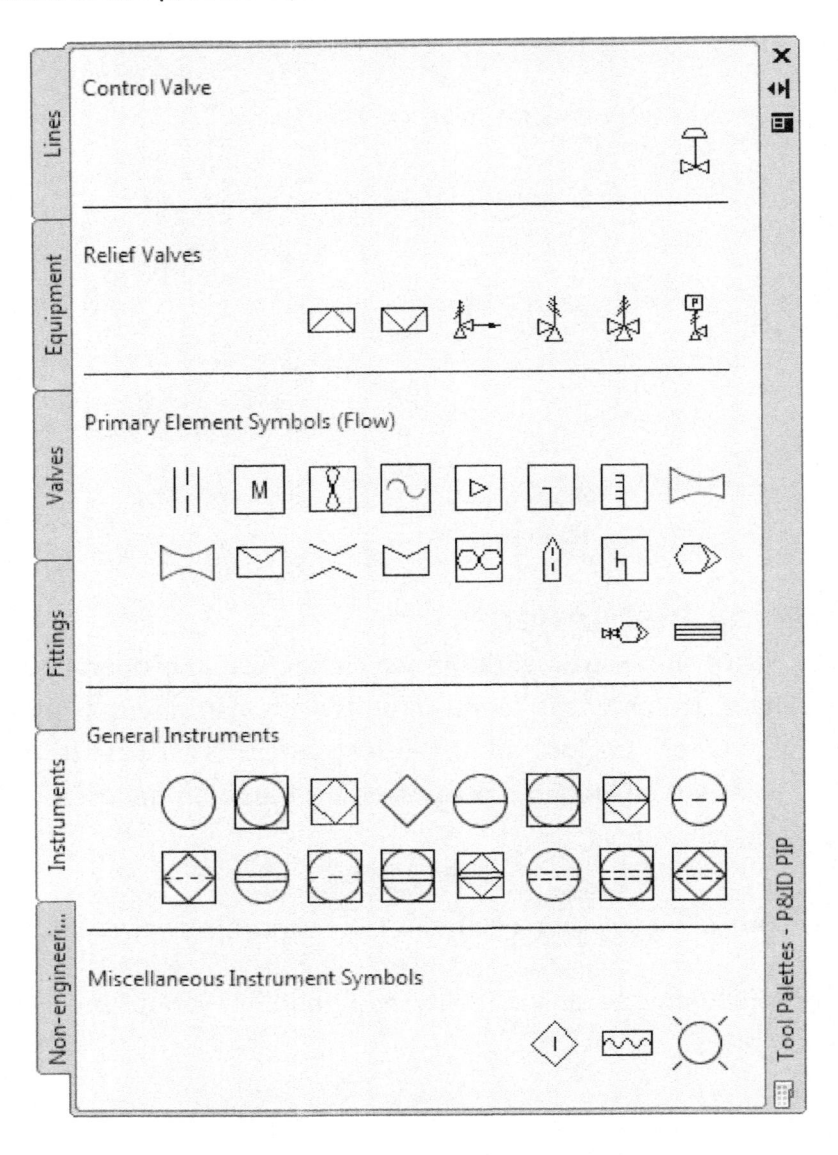

- To place a control valve, click the **Control Valve** icon on the **Valves** tool palette.

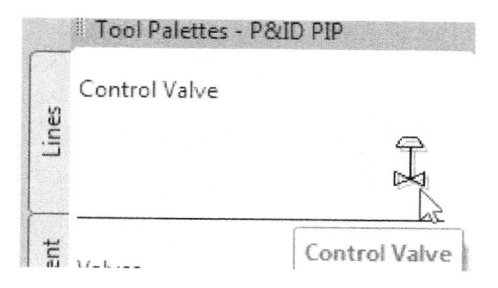

The **Control Valve Browser** appears.

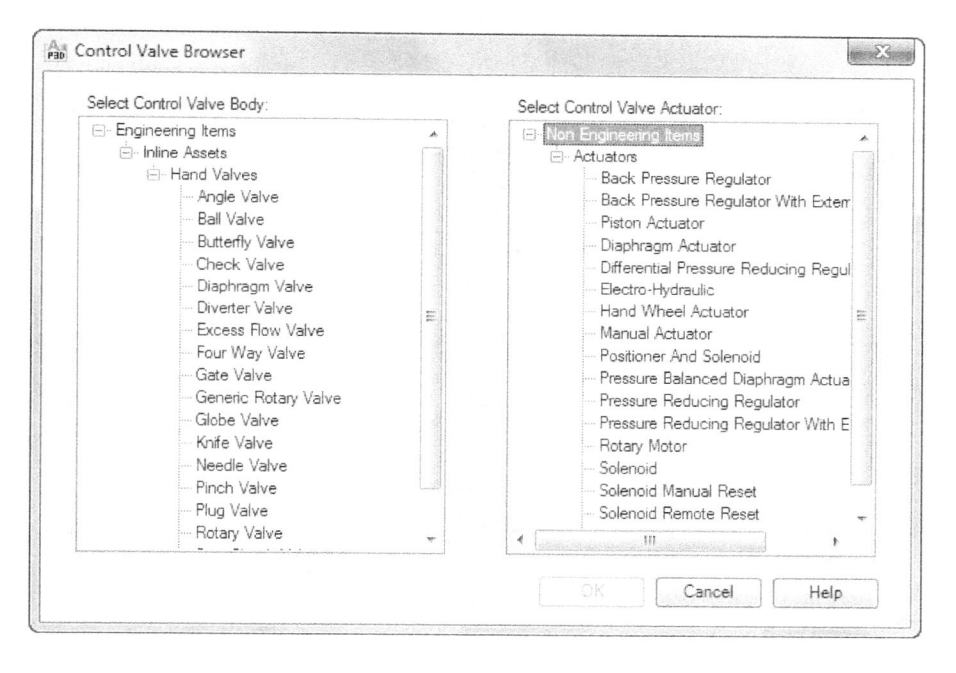

If the **Control Valve Browser** does not appear, select the **Change body or actuator** option from the Command Prompt.

- In the **Control Valve Browser**, select **Gate Valve** as the **Control Valve Body**.

Select Control Valve Body:

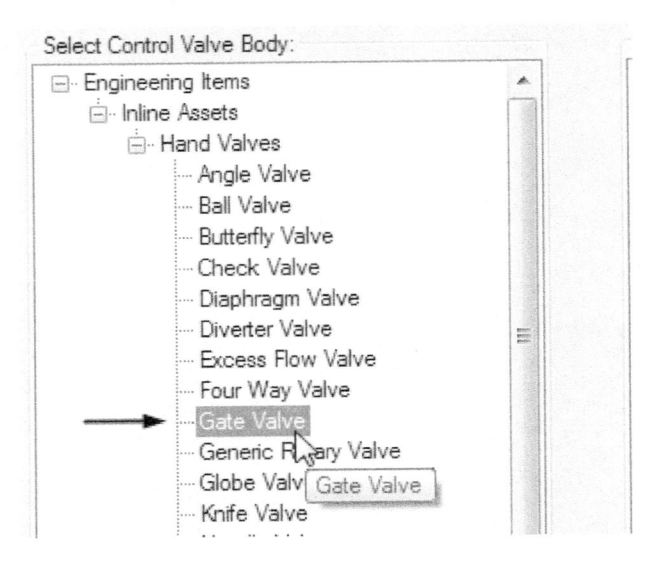

```
Engineering Items
  Inline Assets
    Hand Valves
      Angle Valve
      Ball Valve
      Butterfly Valve
      Check Valve
      Diaphragm Valve
      Diverter Valve
      Excess Flow Valve
      Four Way Valve
  ➤   Gate Valve
      Generic Rotary Valve
      Globe Valv[ Gate Valve ]
      Knife Valve
```

- Select **Piston Actuator** as the **Control Valve Actuator**.

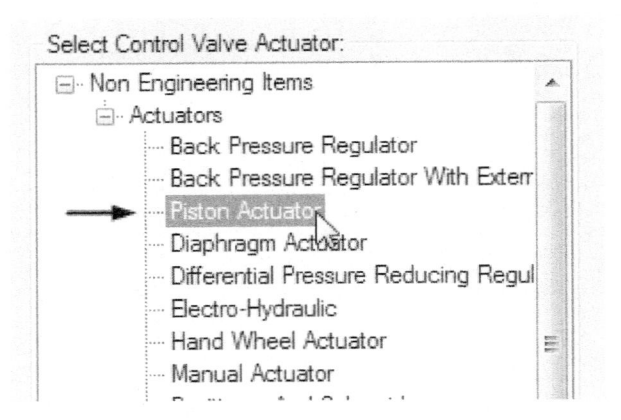

Select Control Valve Actuator:

```
Non Engineering Items
  Actuators
    Back Pressure Regulator
    Back Pressure Regulator With Extern
  ➤ Piston Actuator
    Diaphragm Actuator
    Differential Pressure Reducing Regul
    Electro-Hydraulic
    Hand Wheel Actuator
    Manual Actuator
```

- Click the **OK** button.

- Place the control valve at the location shown in figure.

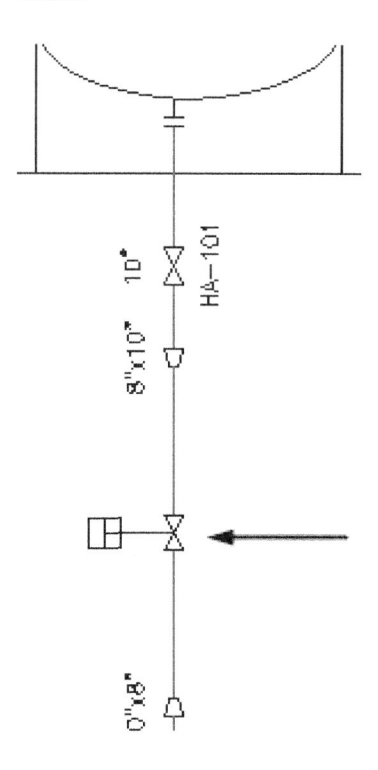

- Place the annotation balloon

The **Assign Tag** dialog appears.

- Specify the values in this dialog.

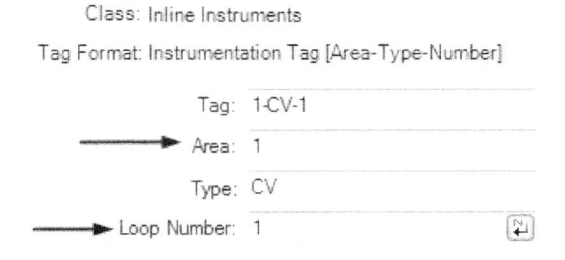

Class: Inline Instruments
Tag Format: Instrumentation Tag [Area-Type-Number]

Tag: 1-CV-1
Area: 1
Type: CV
Loop Number: 1

- Click the **Assign** button.

AutoCAD P&ID Tutorial

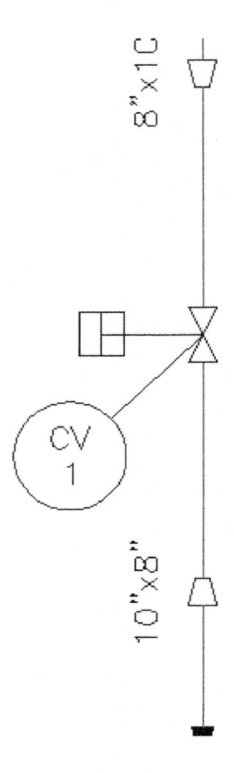

Creating Instrumentation Lines

Instrumentation lines are used to connect the instrument symbols with the P&ID equipment and pipe lines. You can create instrumentation lines by picking them from the **Instrument Lines** section on the **Lines** tool palette.

- To create an electric signal line, click the **Electric Signal** line from the **Instrument Lines** section on the **Lines** tool palette.

AutoCAD P&ID Tutorial

Pipe Lines

Instrument Lines

Electric Signal

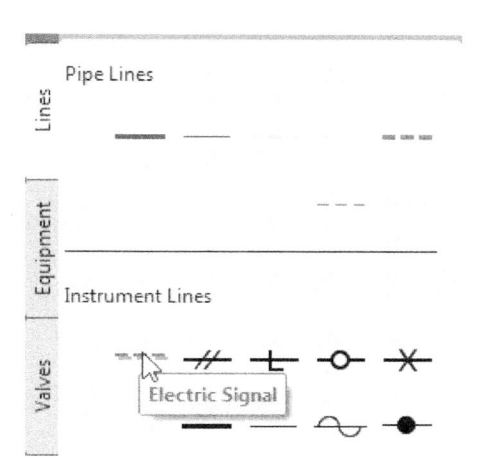

- Select a point on the lower portion of the vessel.

- Move the cursor toward left and select the second point.

- Move the cursor downward and select the third point.

- Move the cursor toward right and select a point on the vessel.

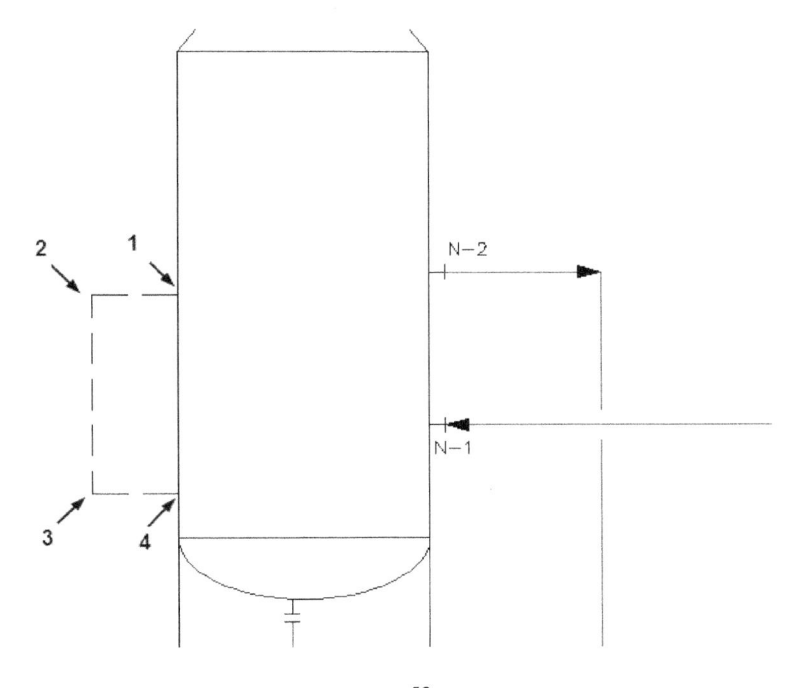

Placing the Field Discrete instrument symbol

- To place a field discrete instrument symbol, click the **Field Discrete Instrument** icon from the **General Instruments** section on the **Instruments** tool palette.

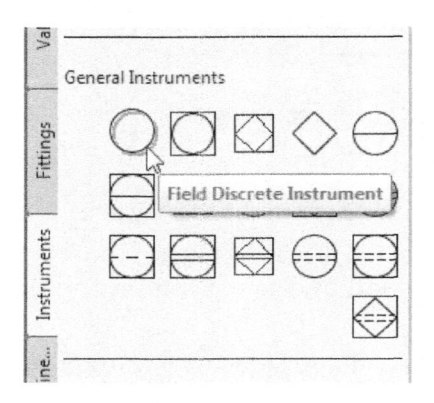

- Place it on the electric signal line.

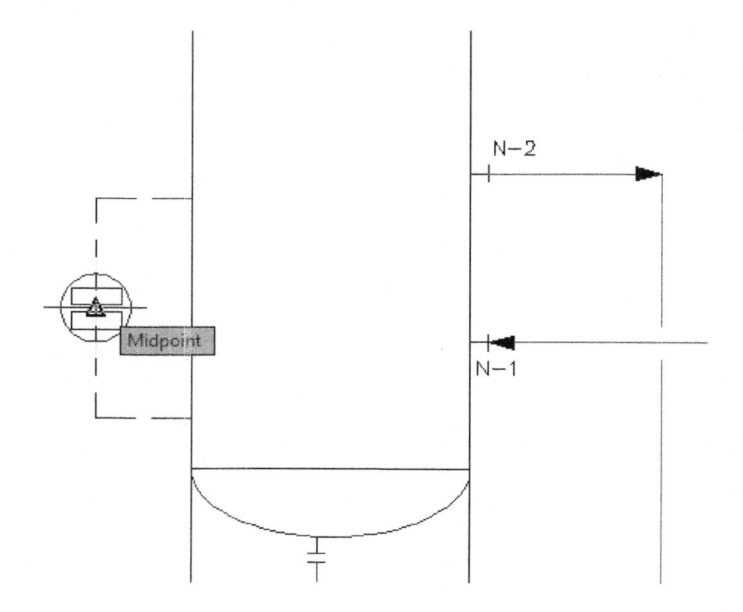

The **Assign Tag** dialog appears.

AutoCAD P&ID Tutorial

- Enter the tag information as shown in figure.

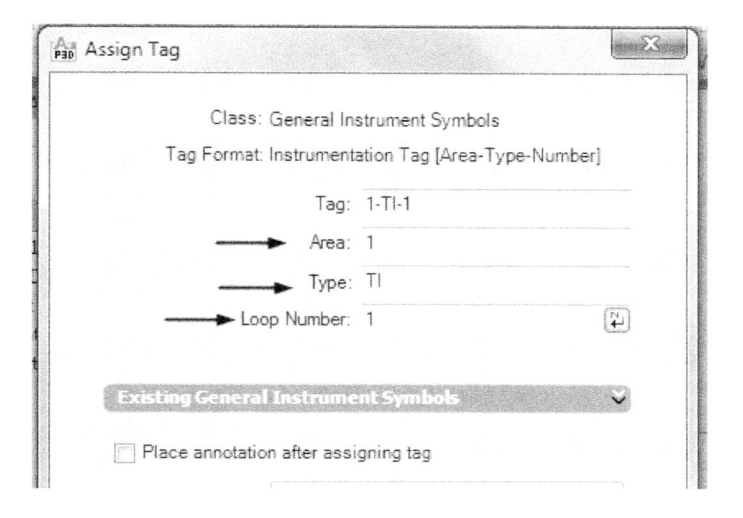

Assign Tag

Class: General Instrument Symbols
Tag Format: Instrumentation Tag [Area-Type-Number]

Tag: 1-TI-1
Area: 1
Type: TI
Loop Number: 1

Existing General Instrument Symbols

☐ Place annotation after assigning tag

- Click the **Assign** button.

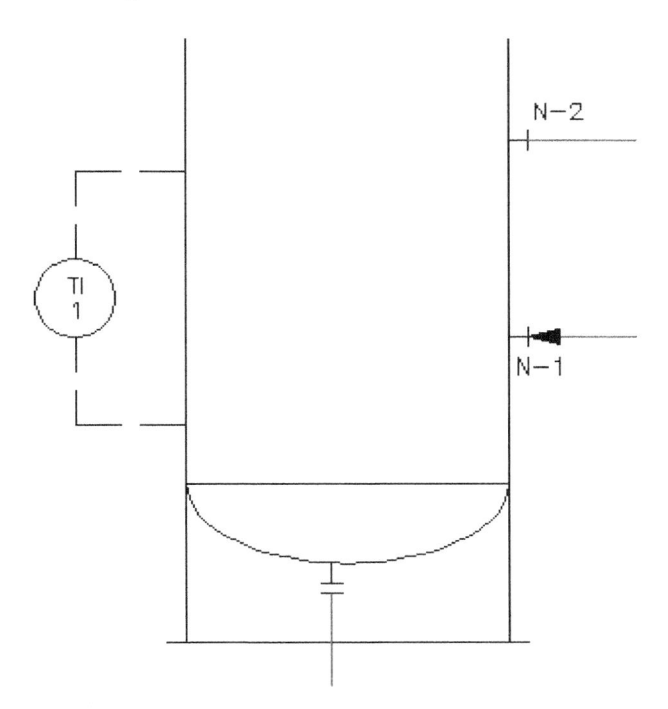

Creating the Pneumatic Signal lines

- To create pneumatic signal lines, click the **Pneumatic Signal** line from the **Instrument Lines** section on the **Lines** tool palette.

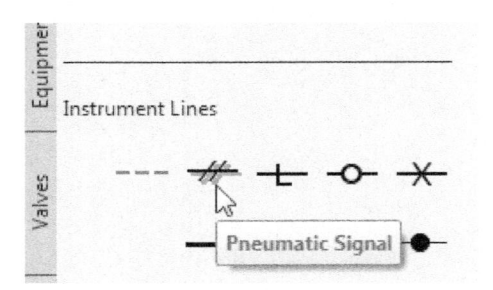

- Select a point on the **Temperature Indicator** symbol.

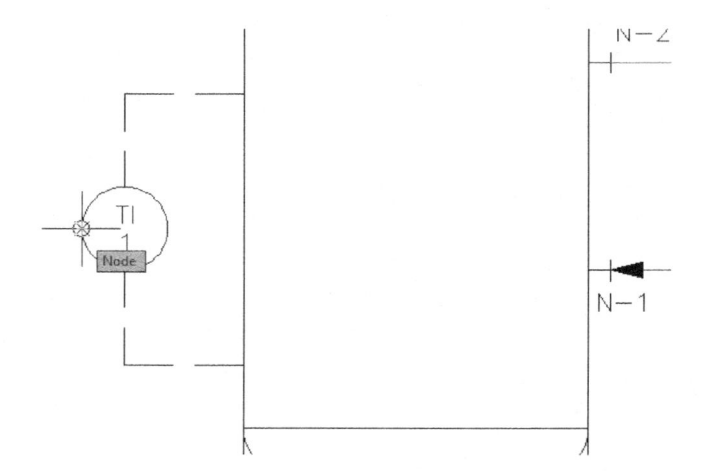

- Connect the signal line with the control valve.

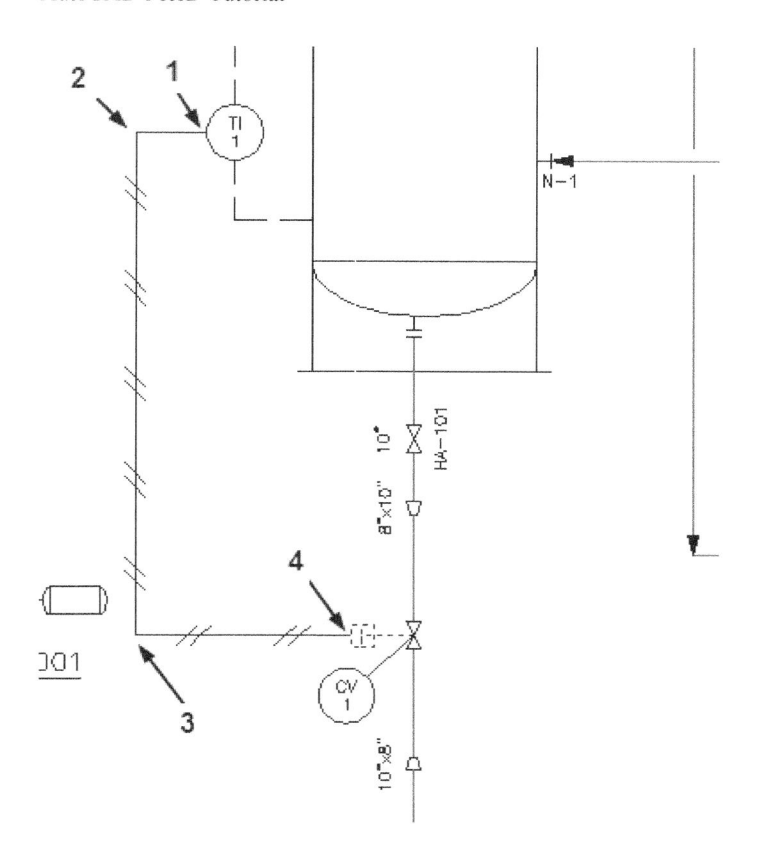

Adding Off page connectors

In this section, you will learn about off-page connectors. Most often, the P&ID of a plant design will be divided into multiple P&ID's. So, you should maintain a connection between the P&ID's. Off page connectors are used to connect the drawings.

- To add an off page connector, click the **Non-engineering** tab on the Tool palette.

Click the **Off Page connector** icon on the **Non-engineering** tool palette.

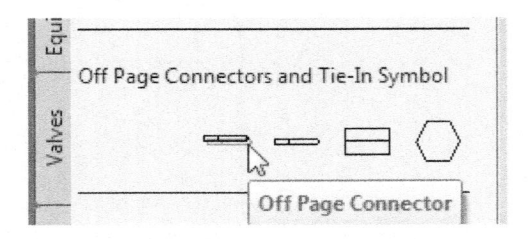

- Select the end point of the line connecting the top portion of the vessel, as shown below.

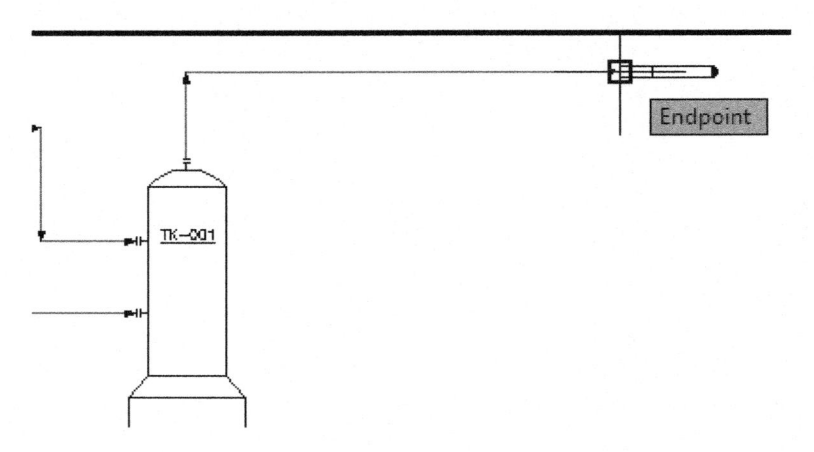

Checking the Drawing

- Click the **Drawing Checker** button on the **Validate** panel of the **Home** Ribbon.

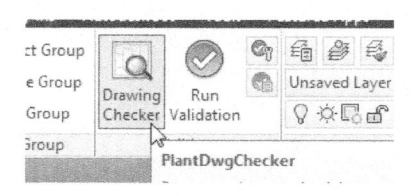

The drawing will be checked for any inconsistencies with the project.

Validating a P&ID

You need to validate a P&ID to check for errors. Before validating a drawing, you need to set the type of errors to be check during validation.

- Click the **Validate Config** button on the **Validate** panel of the **Home** ribbon; the **P&ID Validation Settings** dialog box appears.

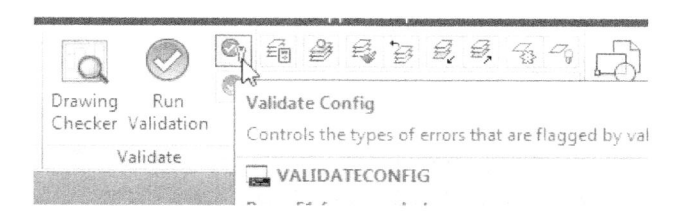

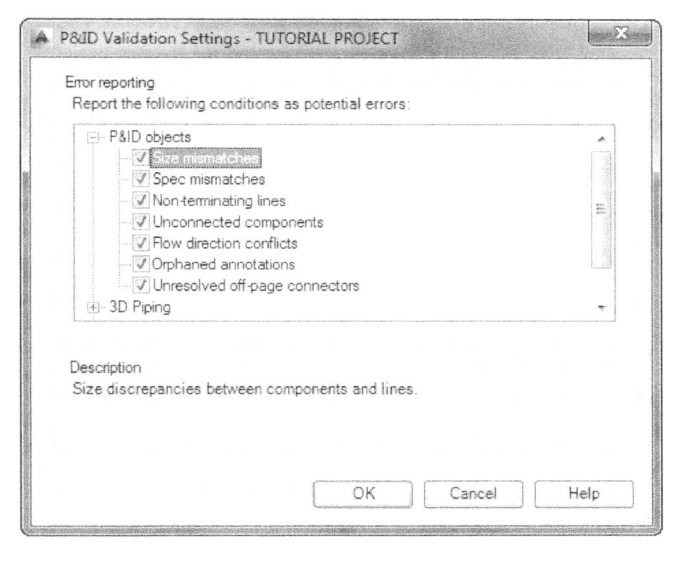

You can select the type of errors to be checked by expanding the **P&ID objects** list. The P&ID will be checked for errors such as size mismatches, spec mismatches, non-terminating lines and so on.

- Click the **OK** button on the **P&ID Validation Settings** dialog box.

- Click the **Run Validation** button on the **Validate** panel of the **Home** Ribbon; the validation will start and **Validation Progress** box appears.

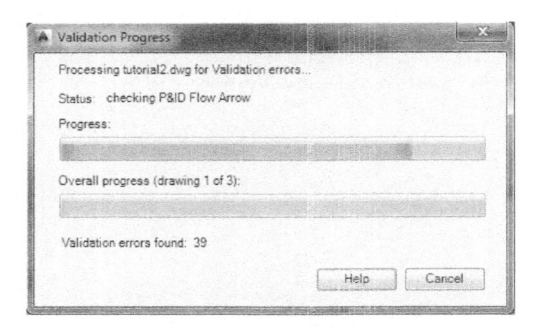

After completing the validation, the **Validation Summary** appears.

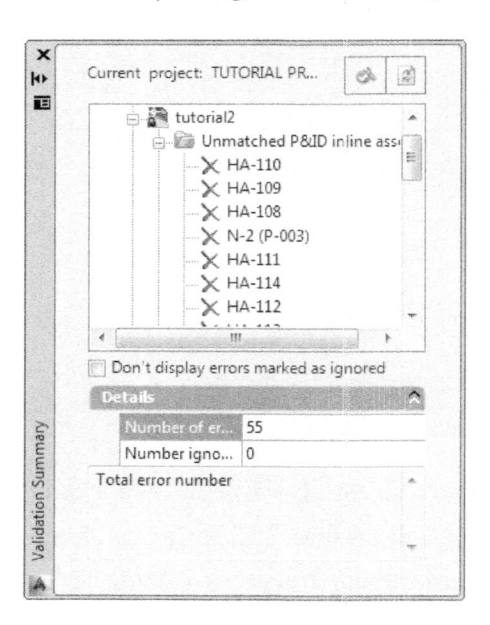

- To zoom to the error location, click on the error in the **Validation Summary**.

AutoCAD P&ID Tutorial

- To ignore the error, right-click on the error and click **Ignore**.

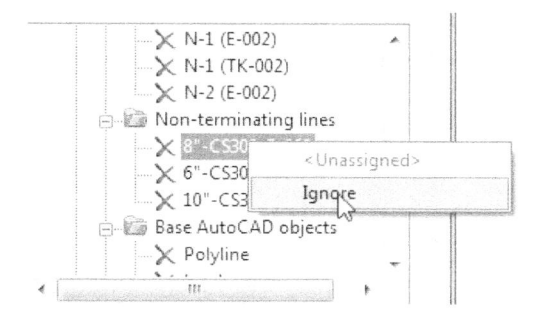

- Click the **Save** button on the **Quick Access Toolbar**.

Tutorial 2

In this tutorial, you will create a P&ID shown in Figure.

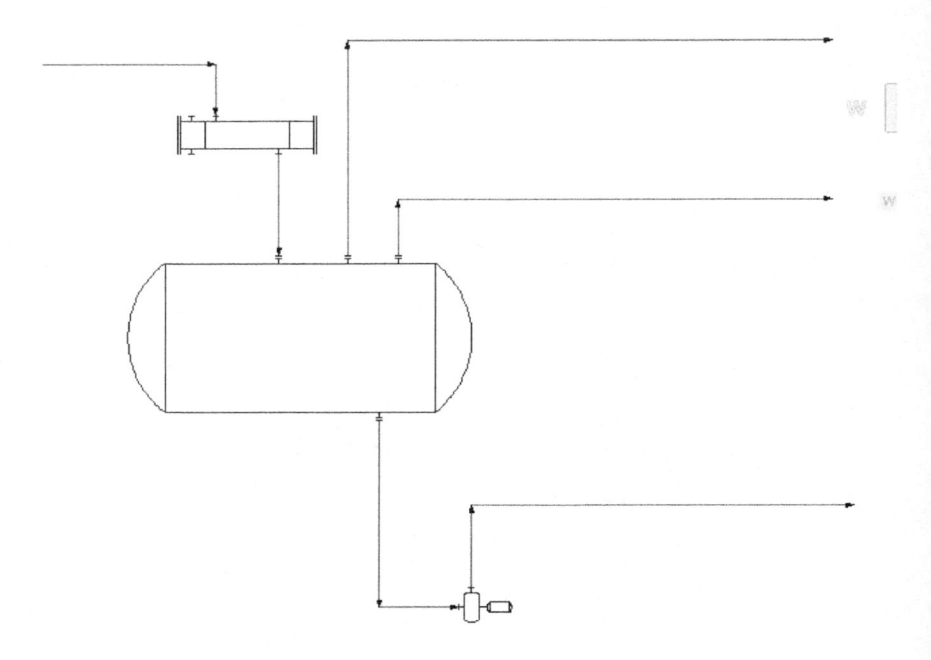

- To create a new P&ID drawing, select the **P&ID Drawings** node in the **Project Manager** and click the **New Drawing** button.

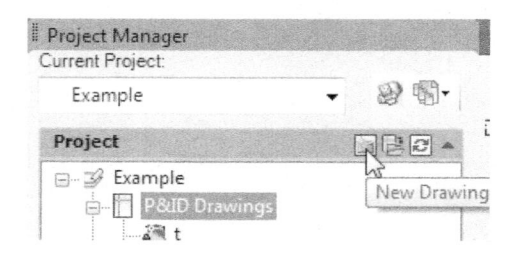

The **New DWG** dialog appears.

- Enter **Tutorial 2** in the **File name** field and click **OK**.

AutoCAD P&ID Tutorial

Creating a Custom symbol and converting it into a P&ID symbol

- Create the symbol shown in below figure using the **Line** and **Arc** tools. Do not dimension it. Dimensions are for your reference only.

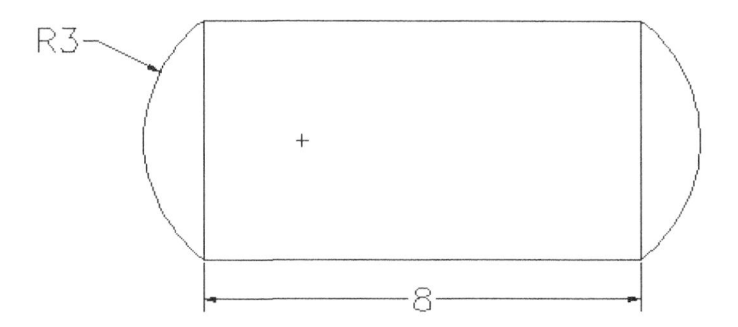

- Select all the entities of the symbol by dragging a window.

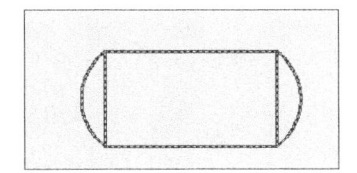

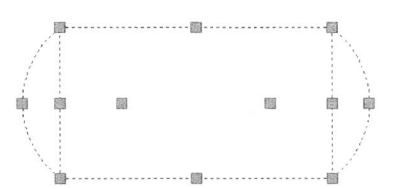

- Right-click and choose **Convert to P&ID Object**.

    The **Convert to P&ID Object** dialog box appears.

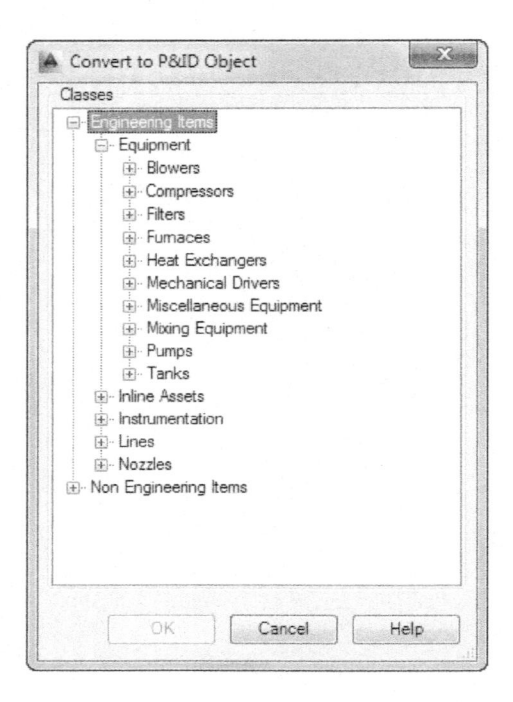

- Expand the **Equipment** class and select **Tank > Vessel**.

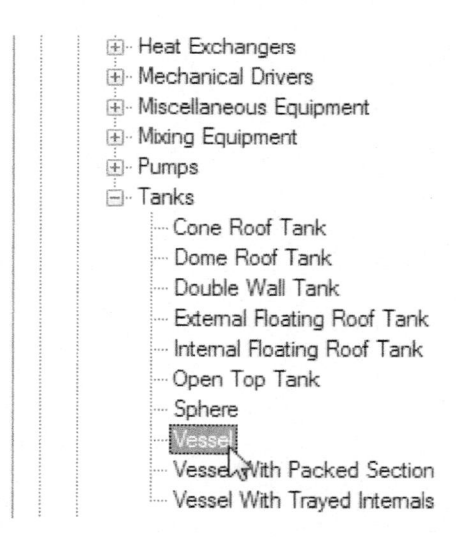

- Click **OK**.

Next, you have to select the insertion base point.

AutoCAD P&ID Tutorial

- Press and hold SHIFT key and right-click.

- Choose **Midpoint** from the shortcut menu.

- Select the midpoint of the lower horizontal line.

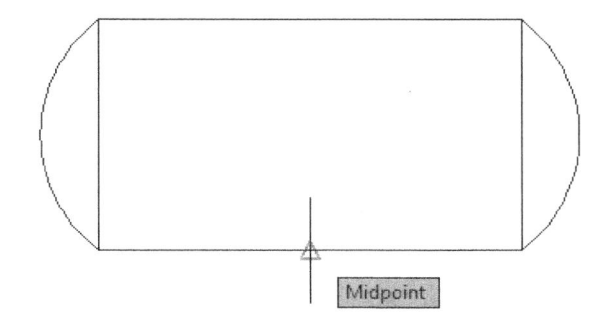

The custom symbol will be converted to a P&ID object.

- Select the symbol and move it to the left side of the drawing sheet.

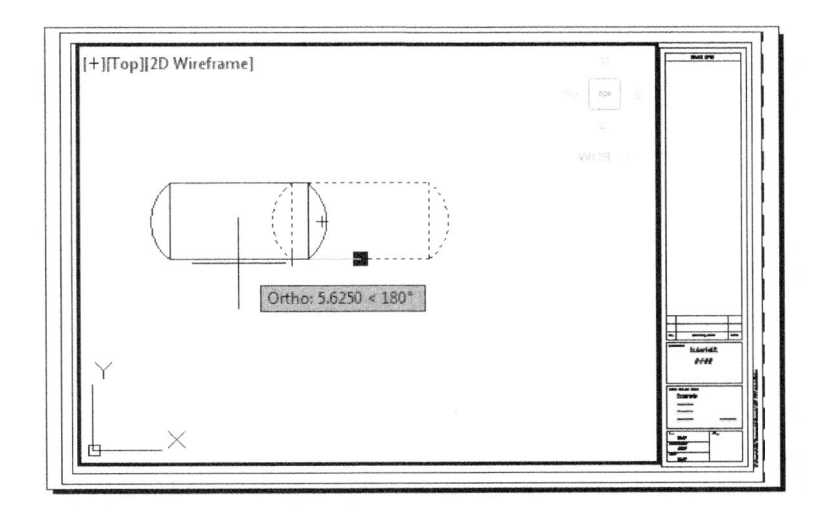

AutoCAD P&ID Tutorial

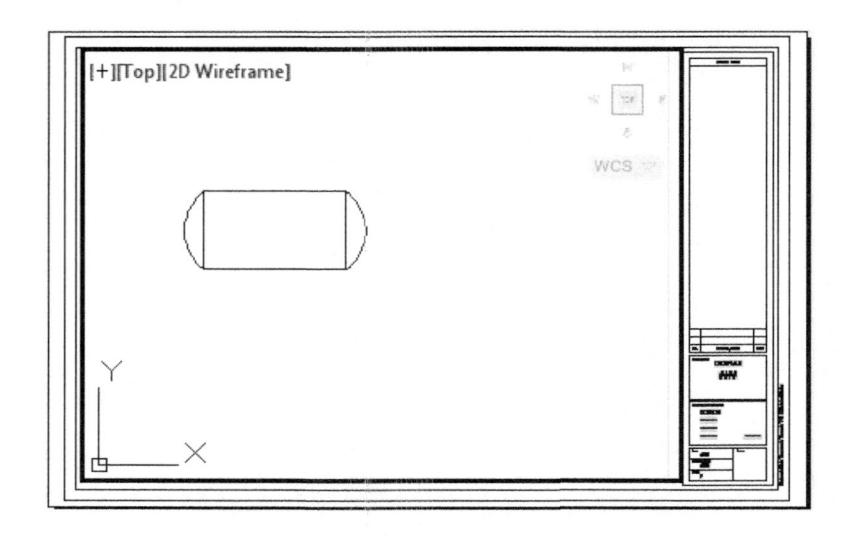

- Place a **TEMA Type NEN Exchanger**.

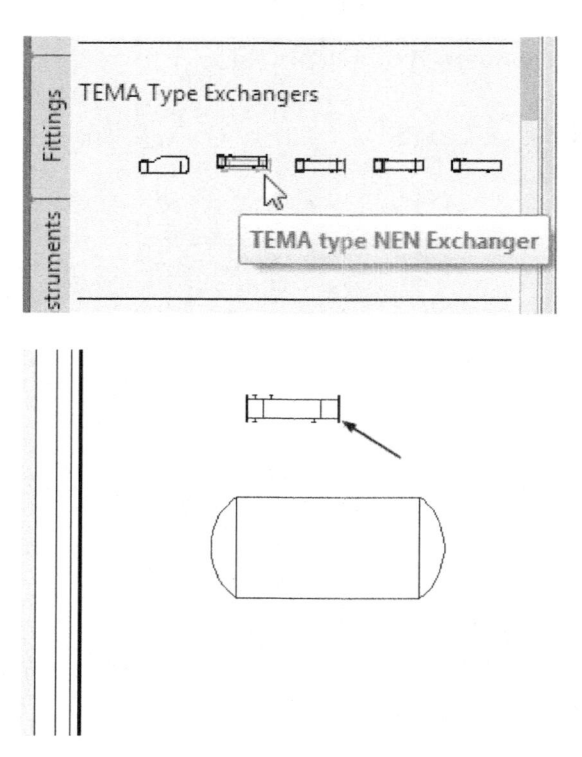

- Place a Centrifugal pump.

65

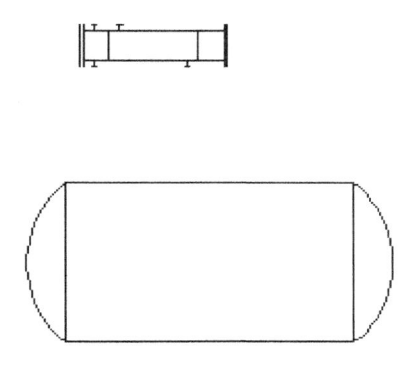

Next, you have to draw the pipe lines.

- Click the **Draw** button on the **Schematic Line** panel of the **Home** ribbon.

- Draw the pipe line connecting the equipment symbols.

AutoCAD P&ID Tutorial

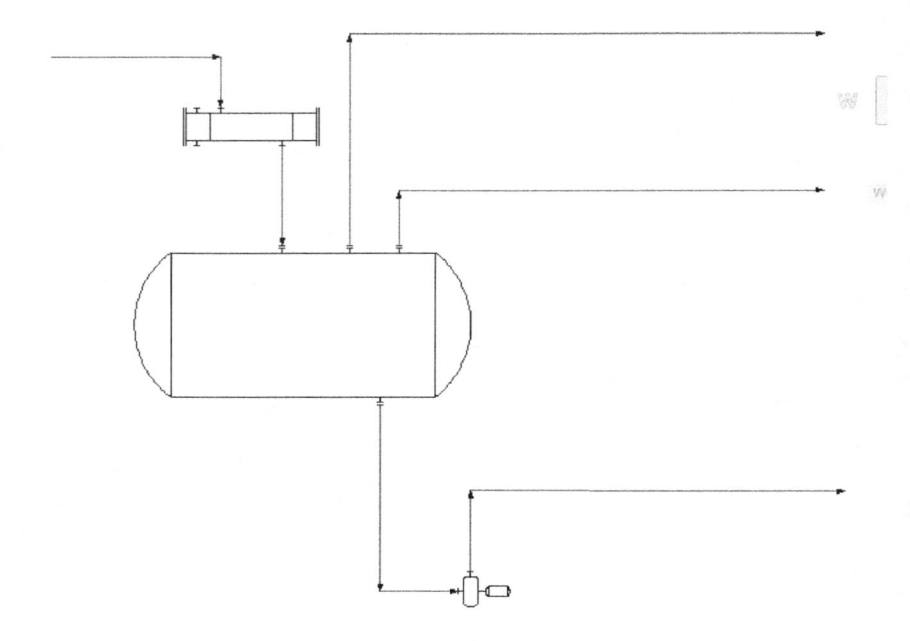

Creating the Secondary Line Segments

- Click the **Secondary Line Segments** icon on the **Lines** tool palette and create the secondary line segments as shown below.

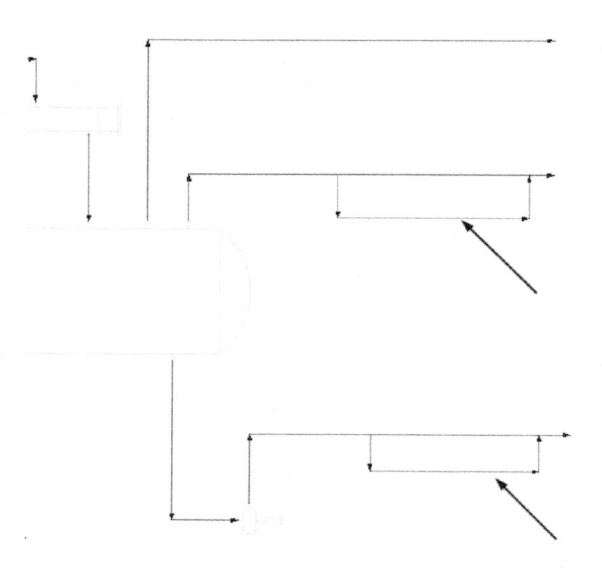

- Click the **Off Page connector** icon on the **Non-engineering** tool palette.

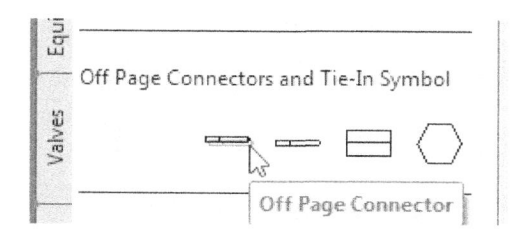

- Select the end point of the line connecting the heat exchanger, as shown below.

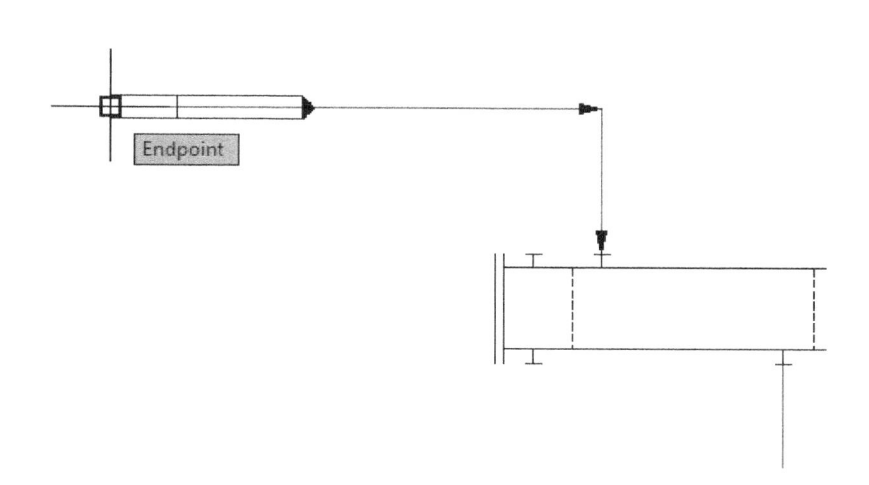

Connecting the Off page connectors

- To connect off page connectors, select the off page connector located at the top left.

- Click on the (+) plus symbol displayed on the off page connector and select **Connect To**.

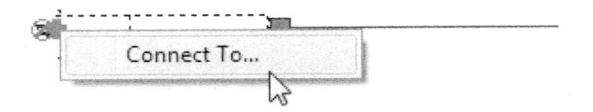

The **Create Connection** window appears.

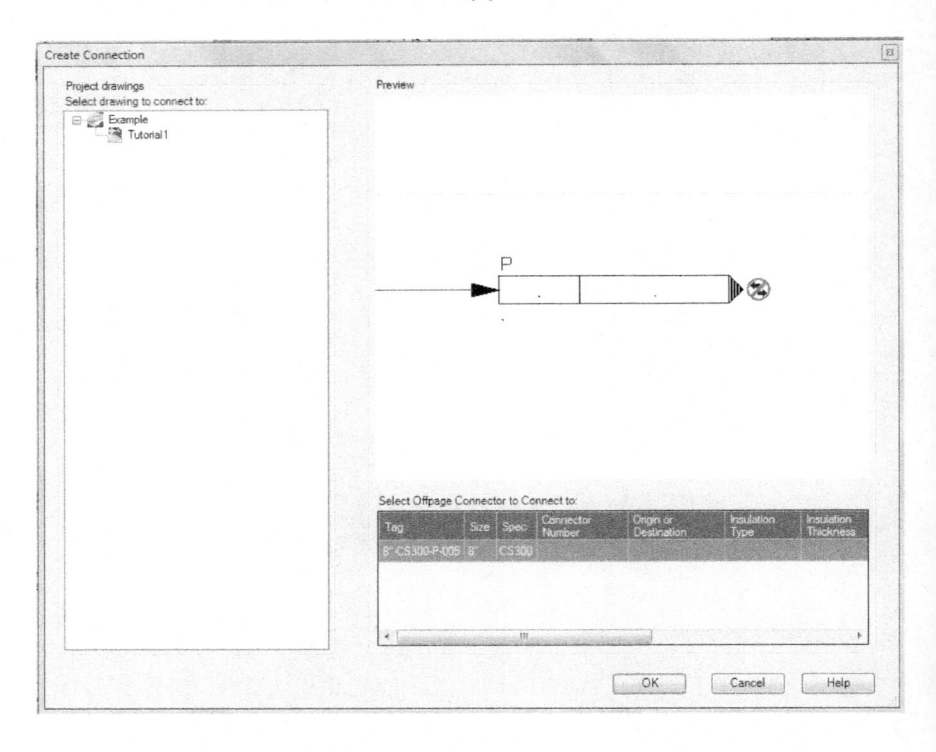

You will notice that the off page connector located in the **Tutorial1.dwg** is selected, by default.

- Click the **OK** button.

The off page connector will connected. But, you will notice that an error symbol is displayed at the end point of the off page connector.

- To solve this error, right-click on the off page connector and select **Off page connector > View connected**.

The **View Connected Off page Connector** dialog box appears.

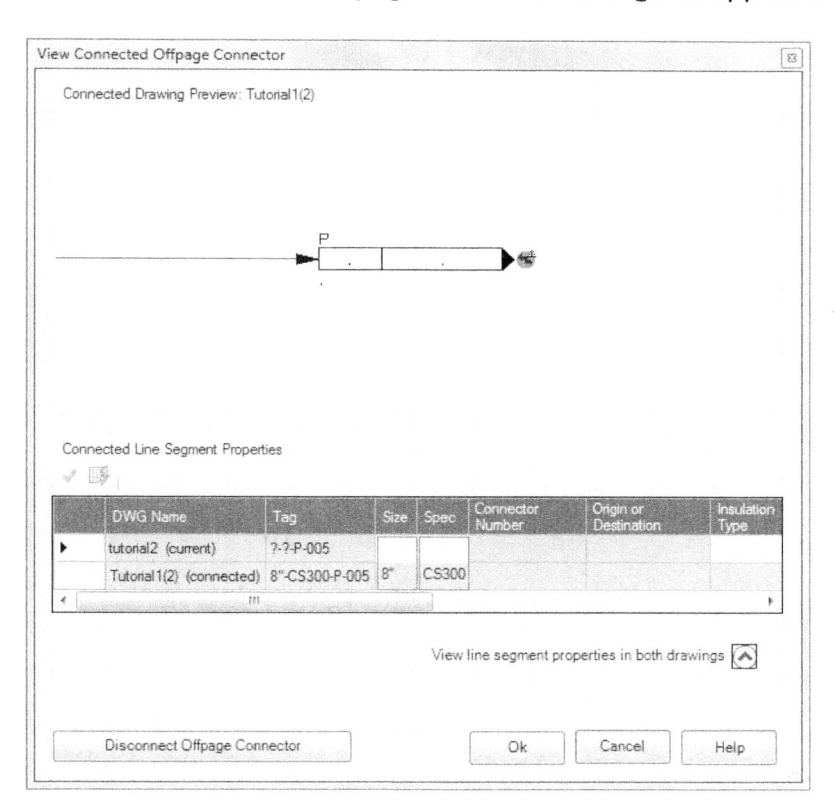

You will notice that the **Size** and **Spec** fields are highlighted in this dialog box. You need to specify the size and spec of the line connected to the off page connector of the **Tutorial2.dwg**.

- Right-click in the **Size** field and select **Accept**.

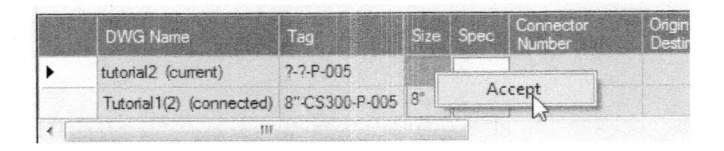

DWG Name	Tag	Size	Spec	Connector Number	Origin Destin
tutorial2 (current)	?-?-P-005				
Tutorial1(2) (connected)	8"-CS300-P-005	8"	Accept		

The sizes of the two lines will be matched.

- Similarly, match the spec.

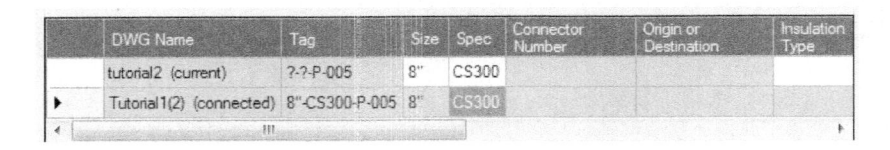

DWG Name	Tag	Size	Spec	Connector Number	Origin or Destination	Insulation Type
tutorial2 (current)	?-?-P-005	8"	CS300			
Tutorial1(2) (connected)	8"-CS300-P-005	8"	CS300			

- Click the **OK** button.

The error will be solved.

- Click the **Save** button on the **Application Menu**.

AutoCAD P&ID Tutorial

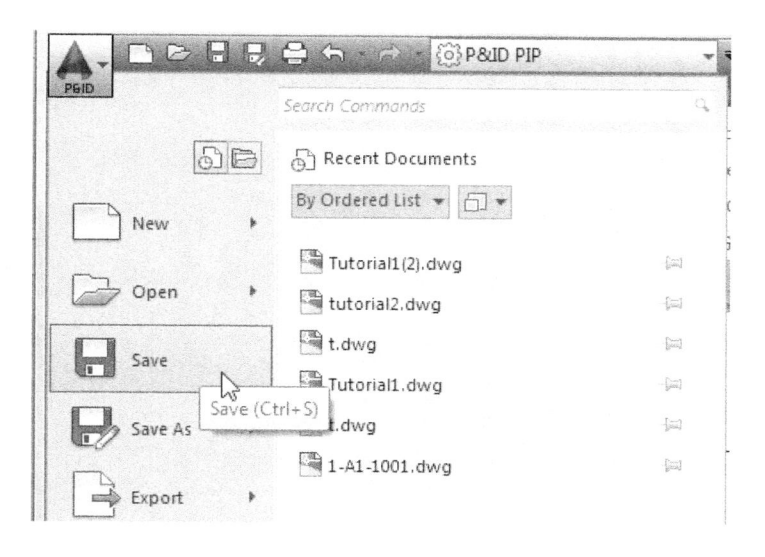

Exercise 1

In this exercise, open the Tutorial2 P&ID and add valves, fittings, instruments and instrumentation lines, and tags. Various regions of the P&ID are given in following figures.

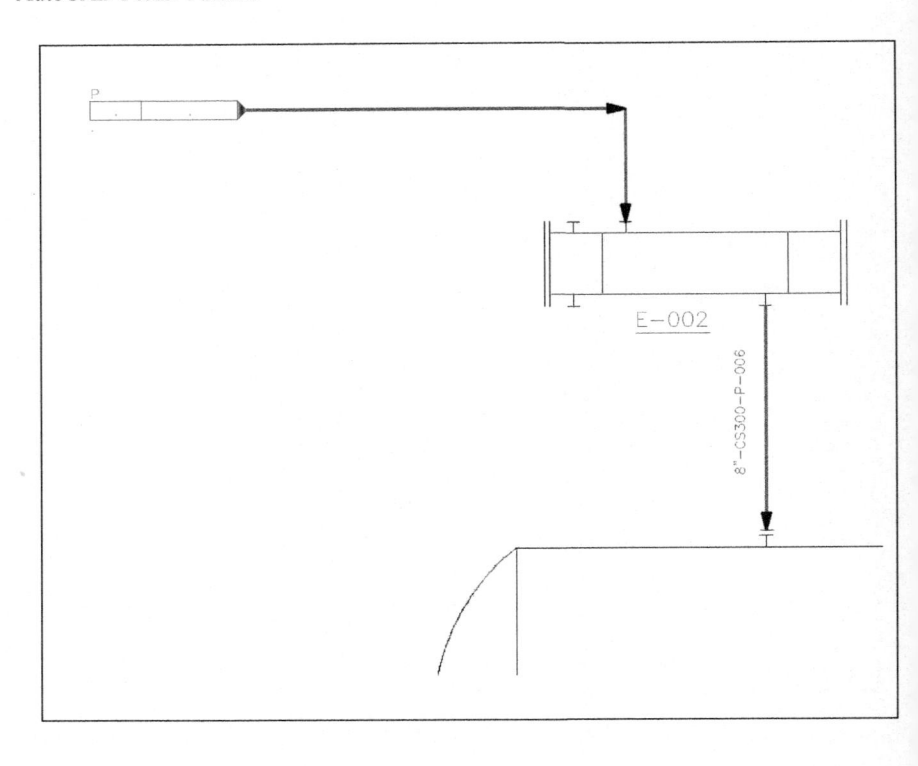

AutoCAD P&ID Tutorial

E-002

8"-CS300-P-006

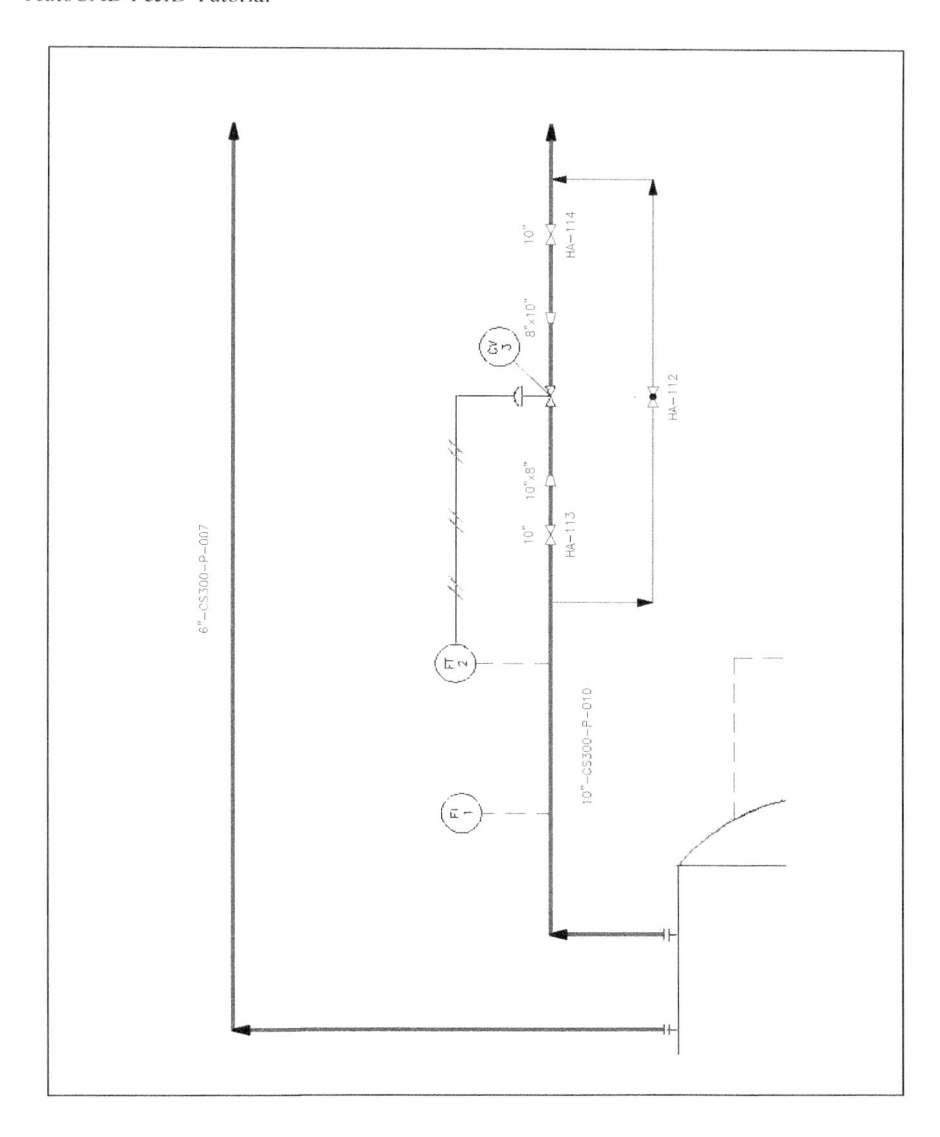

AutoCAD P&ID Tutorial

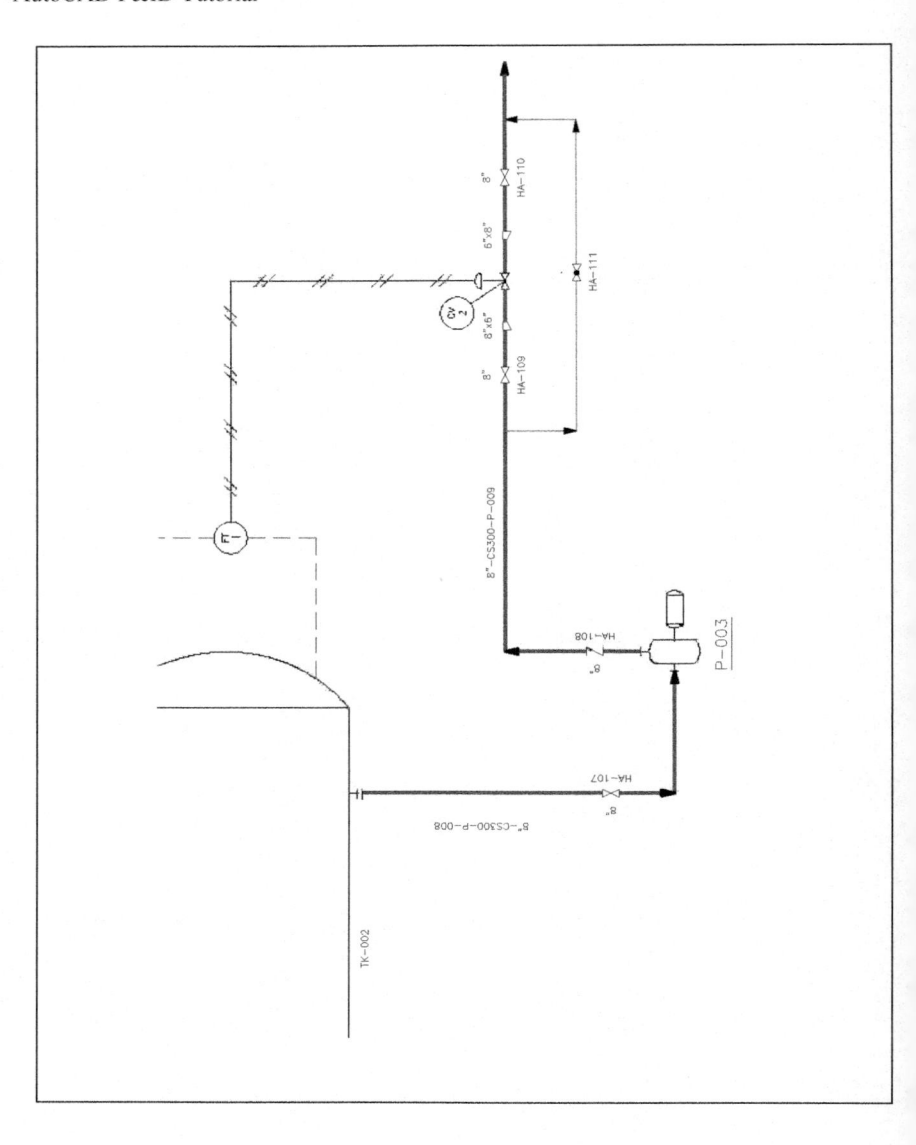

AutoCAD P&ID Tutorial

AutoCAD P&ID Tutorial

The final P&ID of the exercise is given below.

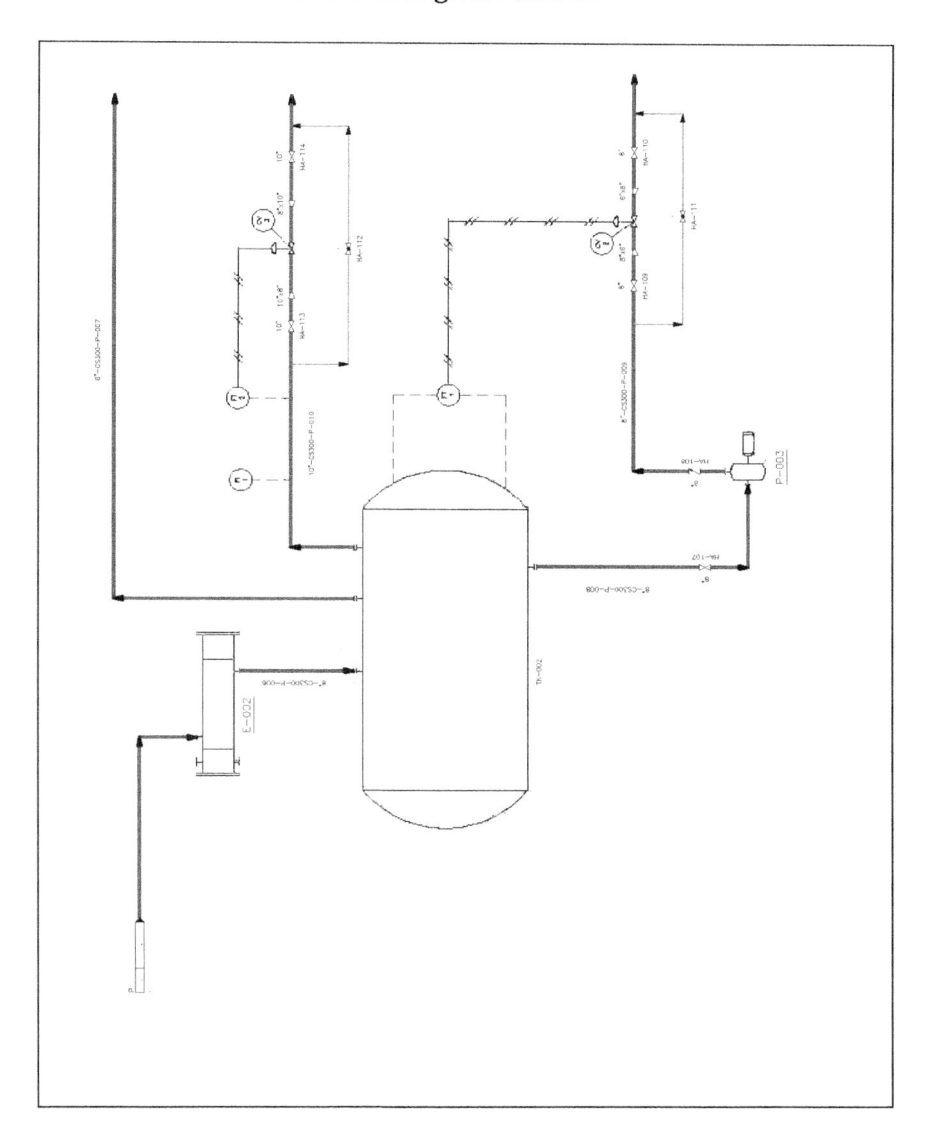

AutoCAD P&ID Tutorial

Tutorial 3 (Editing the P&ID)

In this tutorial, you will open the drawing created in **Tutorial 1** and modify it.

- To open the existing P&ID drawing, right-click on **Tutorial1** in the **Project Manager** and select **Open** from the shortcut menu.

Applying Corners

- To apply corners to a line, select the line connecting the bottom of the vessel.

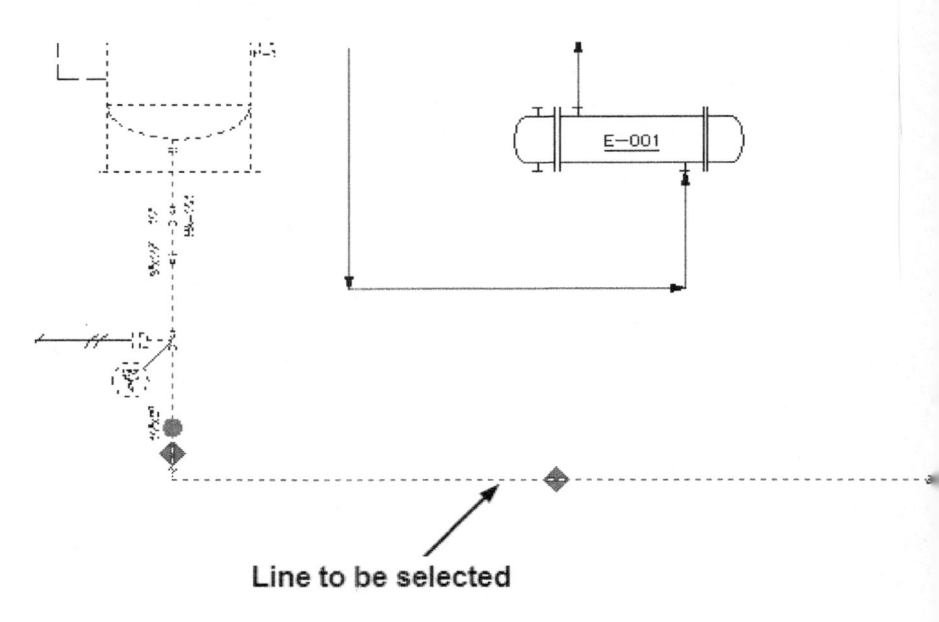

Line to be selected

- Right-click and select **Schematic Line Edit > Apply Corners**.

AutoCAD P&ID Tutorial

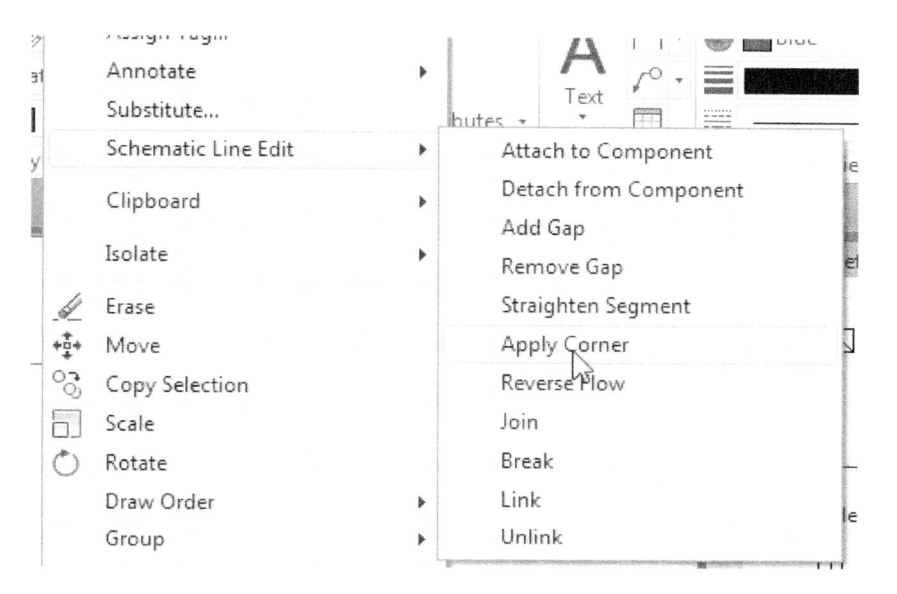

Annotate ▶		
Substitute...		
Schematic Line Edit ▶	Attach to Component	
Clipboard ▶	Detach from Component	
	Add Gap	
Isolate ▶	Remove Gap	
Erase	Straighten Segment	
Move	Apply Corner	
Copy Selection	Reverse Flow	
Scale	Join	
Rotate	Break	
Draw Order ▶	Link	
Group ▶	Unlink	

- Select a point on the line to specify the corner point.

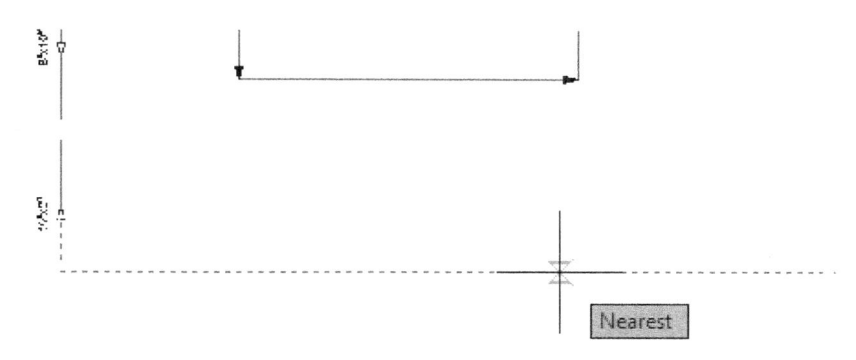

- Move the cursor downward and click to specify the second point.

AutoCAD P&ID Tutorial

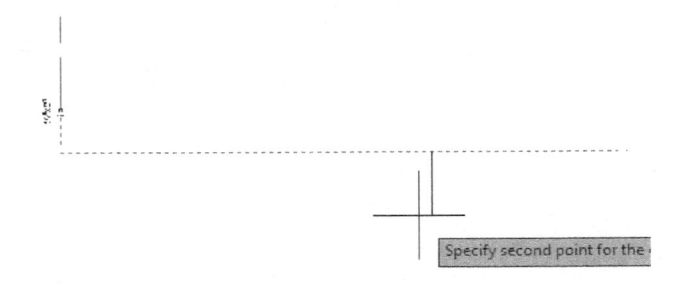

- Select a point on the line to specify the side of the corner.

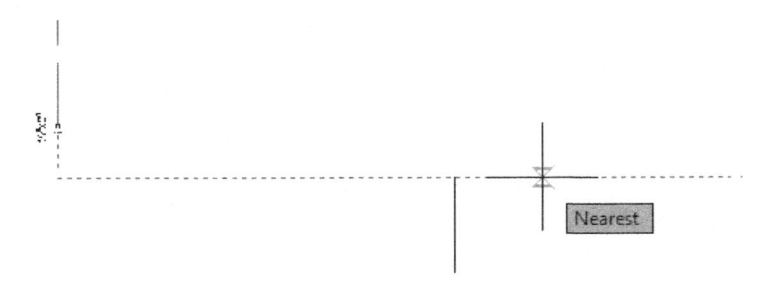

The corner is applied to the line.

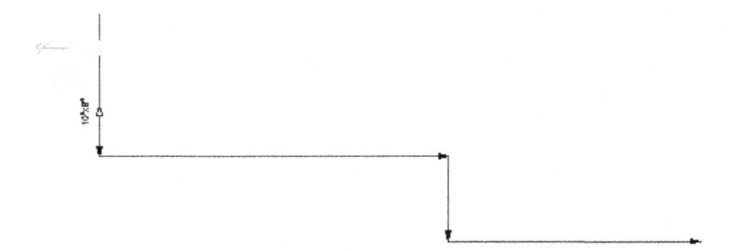

Adding Gaps to lines

In this section, you will add gaps to lines. Before adding gaps, you need to create lines passing over equipment.

- Create two lines passing through the heat exchanger, as shown below.

AutoCAD P&ID Tutorial

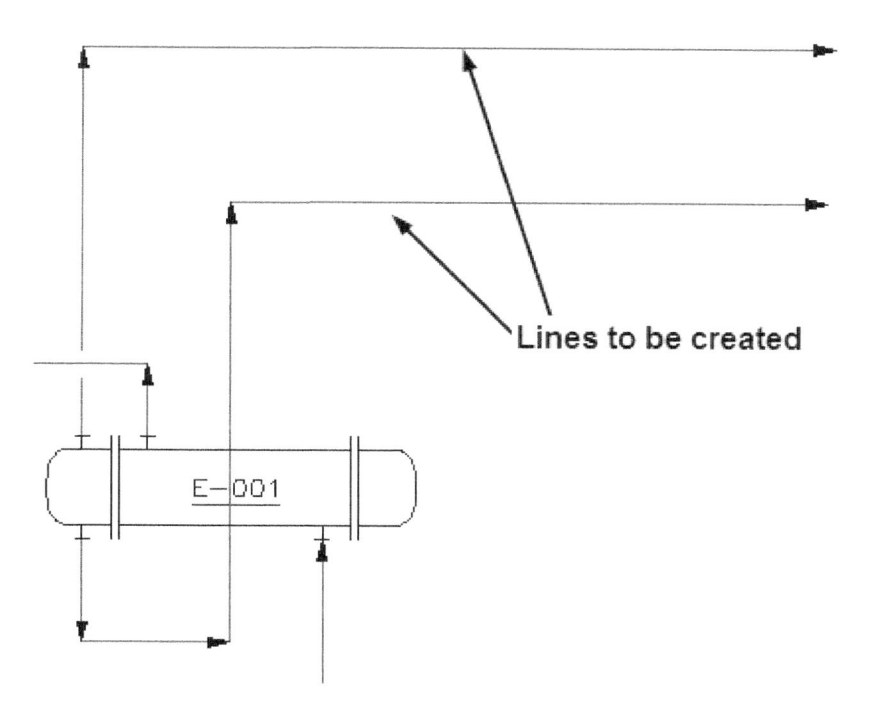

Lines to be created

- Click the **Edit** button on the **Schematic Lines** panel of the **Home** ribbon.

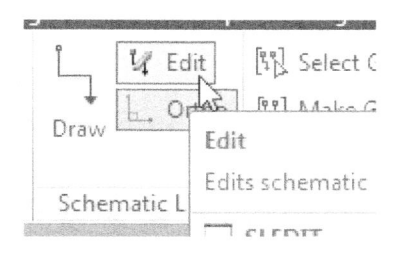

- Select the line passing over the heat exchanger.

AutoCAD P&ID Tutorial

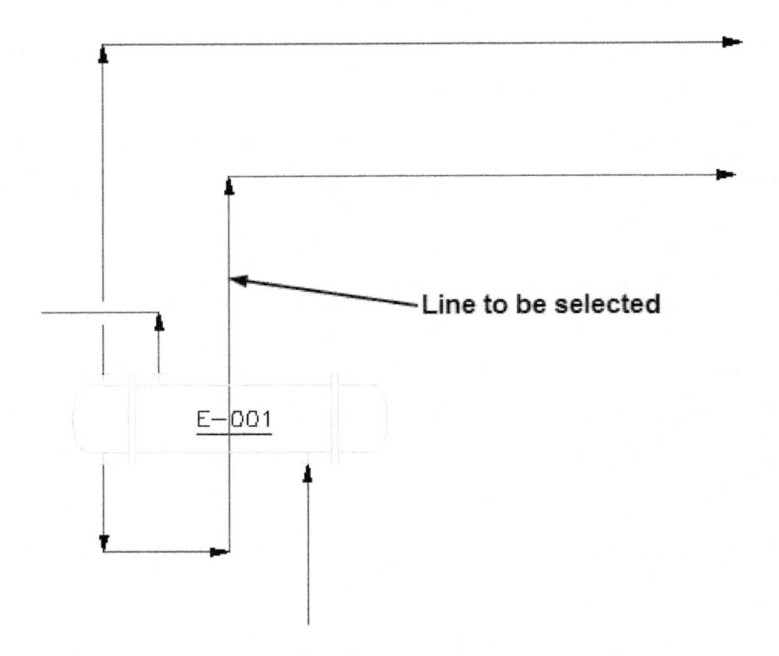

Line to be selected

E—001

- Select the **Gap** option.

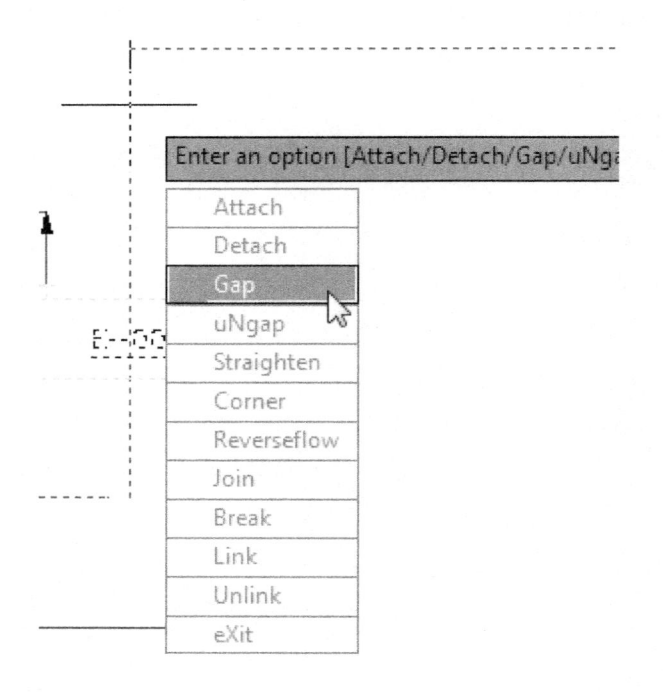

Enter an option [Attach/Detach/Gap/uNgap

- Attach
- Detach
- **Gap**
- uNgap
- Straighten
- Corner
- Reverseflow
- Join
- Break
- Link
- Unlink
- eXit

AutoCAD P&ID Tutorial

- Select the first point of the gap.

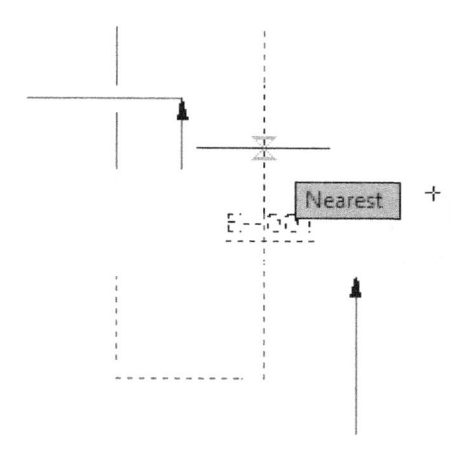

- Select the second point of the gap.

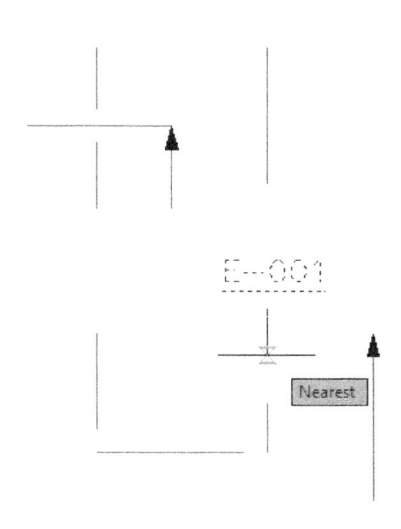

- Press **Enter** key to create the gap.

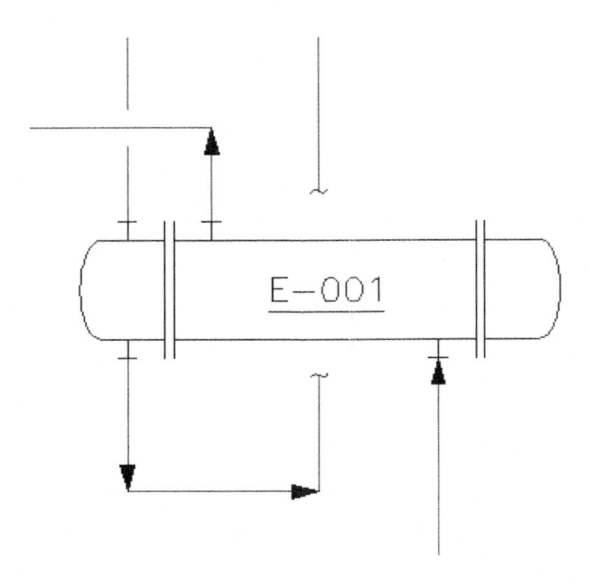

Reversing the Flow Direction

Sometimes you may create line with wrong flow direction. For example, the line connecting the heat exchanger is created with the opposite flow direction, see figure below.

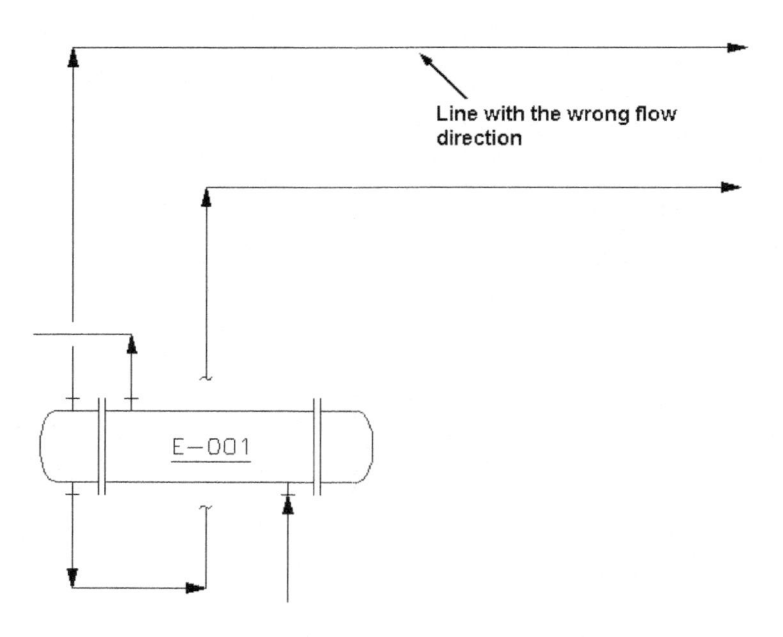

- To reverse the flow direction, select the line, right-click and select **Schematic Line Edit > Reverse Flow**.

The flow direction of the line is reversed.

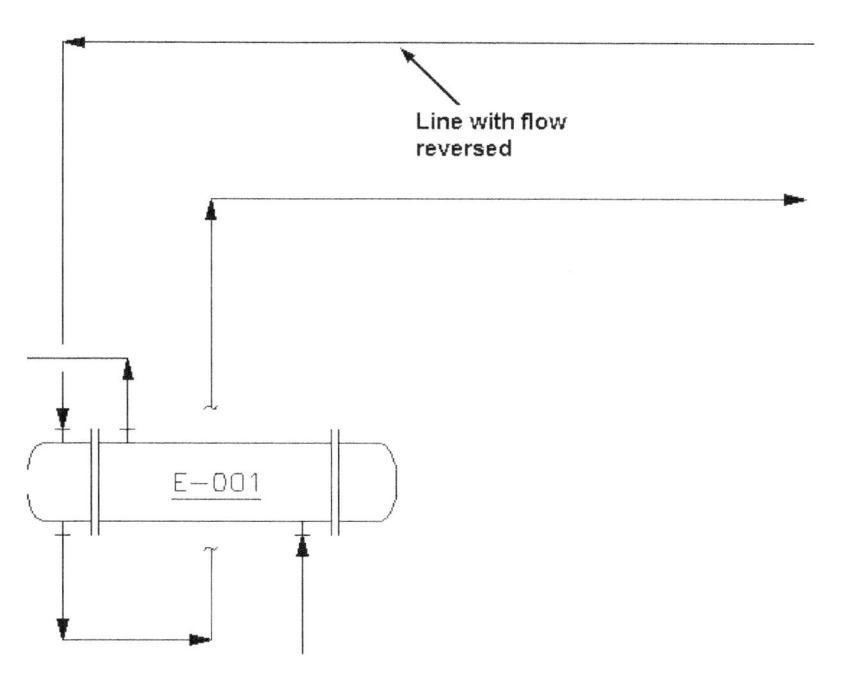

Line with flow reversed

Modifying the lines using grips

In AutoCAD P&ID, you can modify a line using the grips displayed on it.

- To modify the line using grips, select the line; the Move Schematic line grips appears at the midpoint of the line.

AutoCAD P&ID Tutorial

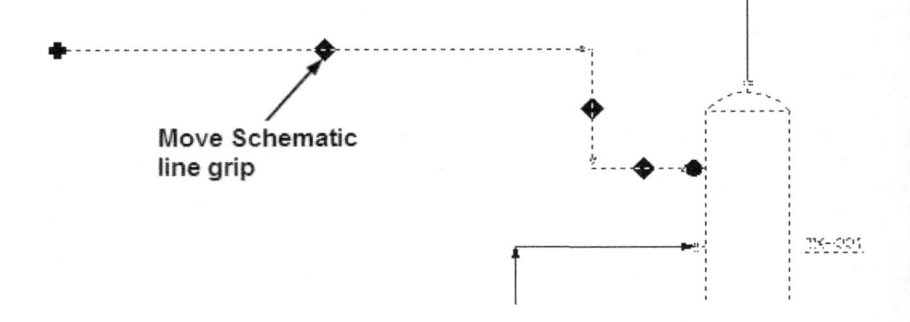

- Select the Move Schematic line grip and move the line downwards.

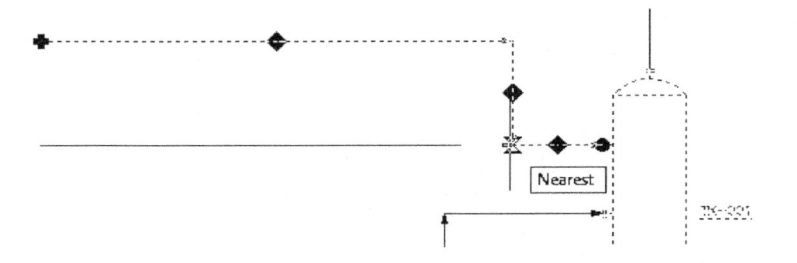

- Select the point in line to the nozzle. The line is modified.

- To disconnect the line from a P&ID component, select the Connection point grip displayed on the line and move the cursor away from the component. The line will be detached from the component.

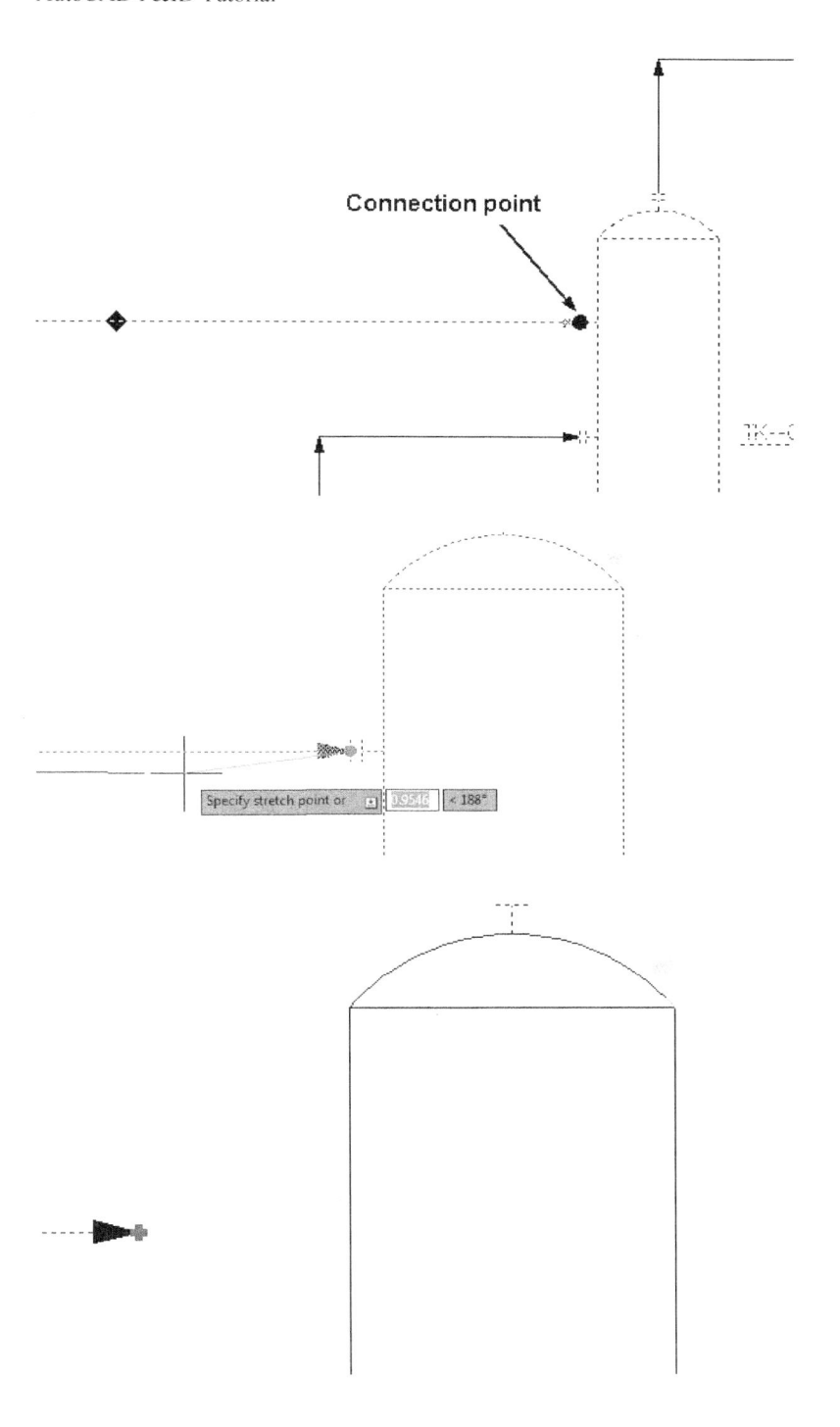

AutoCAD P&ID Tutorial

Connection point

Specify stretch point or 0.9548 < 188°

AutoCAD P&ID Tutorial

Note: You can also detach a line from a component by using the **Detach** option. To do so, right-click on the line and select **Schematic Line Edit > Detach from component**.

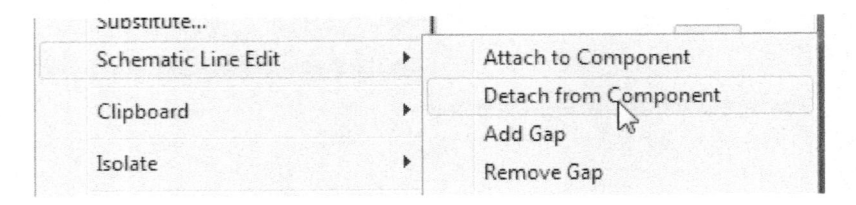

- To reattach the line to the component, click on the **Continue grip** and connect it to the component.

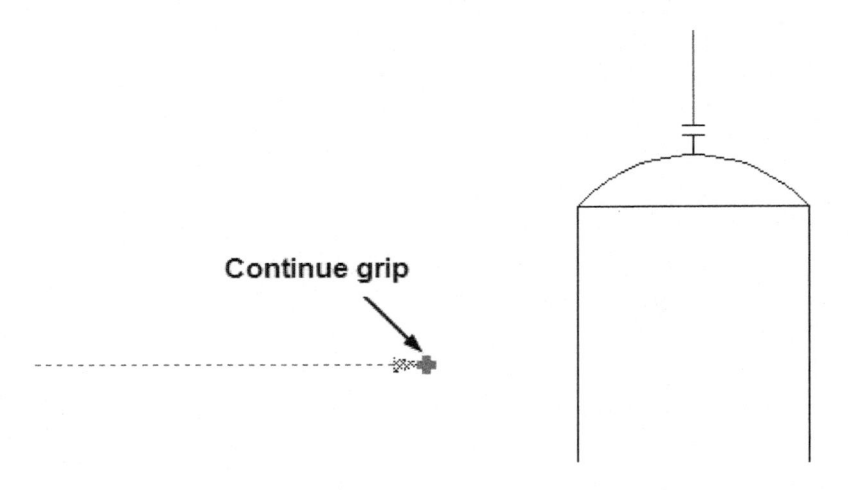

You can also attach a line to the component by selecting **Schematic Line Edit > Attach to Component**.

Substituting the Symbols

In AutoCAD P&ID, you can change the symbols by substituting them with another symbol of the same group.

- To substitute a valve symbol, select the **Check valve** placed on the line connecting the centrifugal pump.

The Substitute grip appears on it.

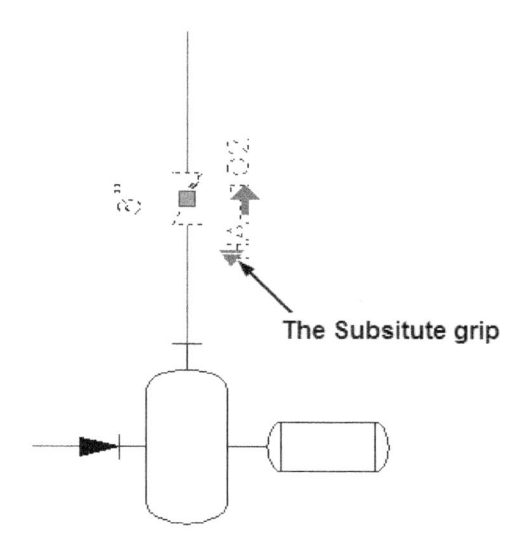

- Click on the substitute grip to display various valve symbols.

- Select the Globe Valve.

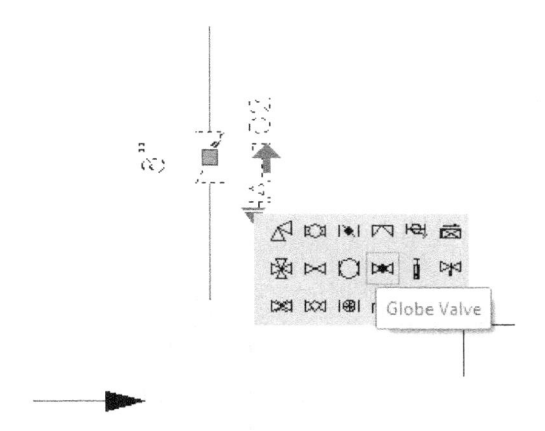

The Globe valve will replace the Check Valve.

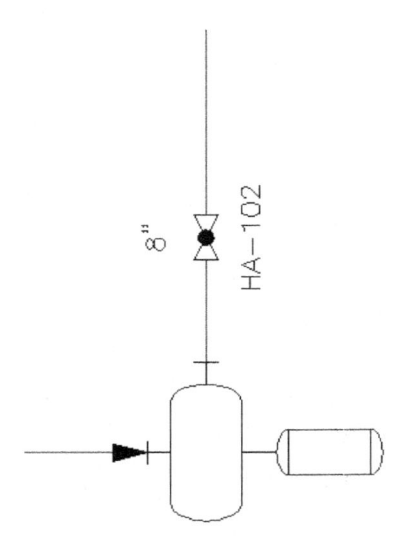

- To substitute an instrument symbol, select the Temperature Indicator symbol connected to the vessel.

- Click the Substitute grip.

- Select **Primary Accessible DCS**.

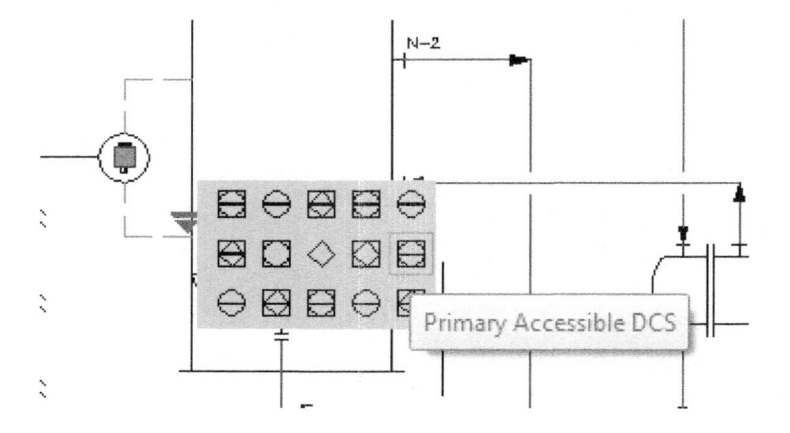

The instrument symbol will be replaced.

AutoCAD P&ID Tutorial

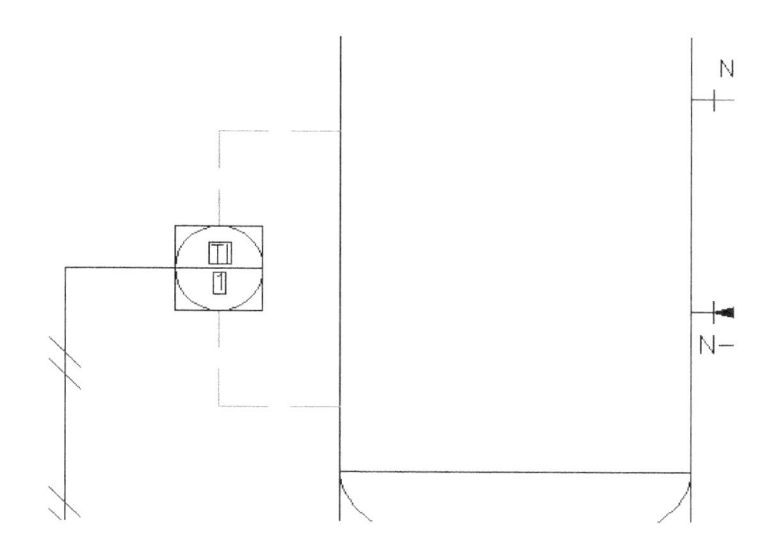

You can also substitute equipment symbols. But, you have to reconnect the pipe lines. For example, on substituting a centrifugal pump with a vertical inline pump, the pipe line will be disconnected. You need to again connect the pipelines using the grips.

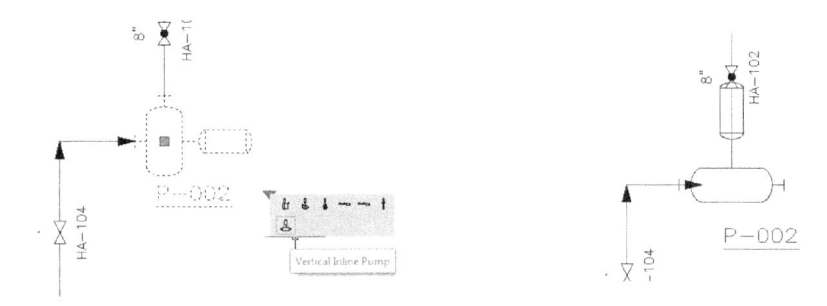

- Save the P&ID drawing. Do not close it.

Tutorial 4 (Managing Data)

In this tutorial, you will learn to view, export and import P&ID data. You need to use the Data Manager to view, export or import data. To invoke the Data Manager, click the **Data Manager** button on **Project** panel of the **Home** ribbon.

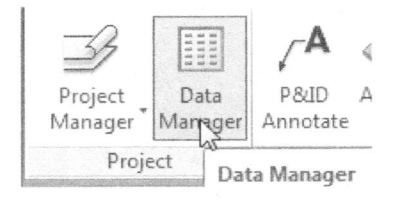

The **Data Manager** appears as shown in figure. Various components of the **Data Manager** are shown in the figure.

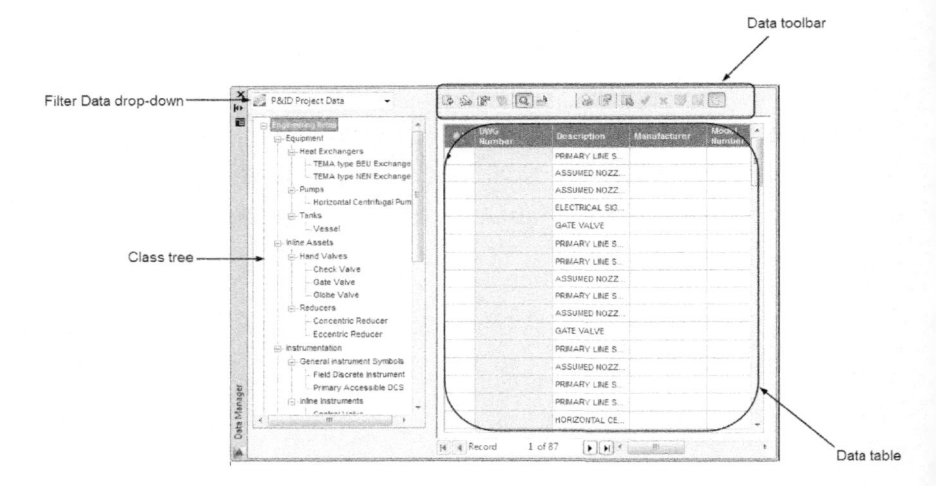

The **Filter Data** drop-down is used to select the type of data to be displayed in the **Data Manager**. You can select the **Current Drawing Data**, **P&ID Project Data** or the **Project Reports**.

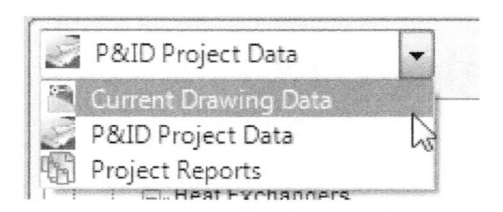

The **Class** tree is used to select the required P&ID class. The data related to the selected class will be displayed.

The **Data Manager** toolbar is used to perform various operations such as import, export, view data and so on.

The **Data** table is similar to a spreadsheet and displays data.

Filtering the Data

- Open the **Tutorial1.dwg**, if not already opened.

- Invoke the **Data Manager** by clicking the **Data Manager** button on the **Projects** panel.

- To view the data of the currently opened drawing file, click **Current Drawing Data** on the **Filter data** drop-down.

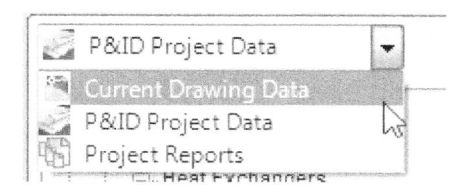

- To view all the equipment in the drawing, click **Equipment** from the **Class** tree.

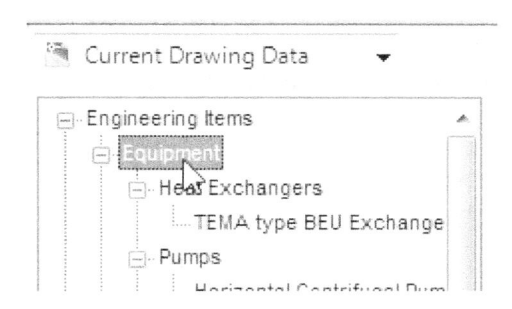

All the equipment data appears in the Data table.

Tag	Type	Description	Manufacturer	Model Number
P-001	P	HORIZONTAL CE...		
TK-001	TK	VESSEL		
P-002	P	HORIZONTAL CE...		
E-001	E	TEMA TYPE BEU ...		

- To view the nozzle data, click **Nozzles** in the **Class** tree.

The nozzle data will appear in the Data table.

Tag	Size	Spec	Description	Manufacturer	Model Number
N-2	?	?	ASSUMED NOZZ...		
N-2	10"	CS300	ASSUMED NOZZ...		
N-1	?	?	ASSUMED NOZZ...		
N-1	8"	CS300	ASSUMED NOZZ...		
N-2	?	?	ASSUMED NOZZ...		
N-4	8"	CS300	FLANGED NOZZLE		
N-1	?	?	SINGLE LINE NO...		
N-6	10"	CS300	FLANGED NOZZLE		
N-3	8"	CS300	FLANGED NOZZLE		
N-2	?	?	SINGLE LINE NO...		
N-1	8"	CS300	ASSUMED NOZZ...		
N-3	?	?	ASSUMED NOZZ...		
N-4	?	?	ASSUMED NOZZ...		
N-1	?	?	FLANGED NOZZLE		

- To filter the data, right-click on the **8"** size in the **Size** column and select **Filter By Selection**.

AutoCAD P&ID Tutorial

[Screenshot of data table with right-click context menu showing Cut, Copy, Paste, Zoom, Filter By Selection, Filter Excluding Selection, Filter For:, Remove Filter options. Table rows show N-1, N-2, N-4, N-1, N-6, N-3, N-2, N-1, N-3 with sizes 8", ?, 8", ?, 10", 8", ?, 8", ?]

The nozzle data will be filtered and the Data table displays only the 8"size nozzles.

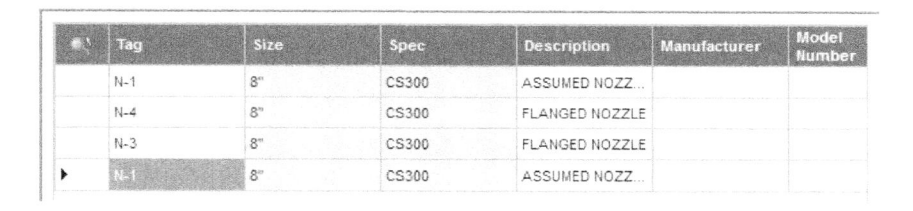

Tag	Size	Spec	Description	Manufacturer	Model Number
N-1	8"	CS300	ASSUMED NOZZ...		
N-4	8"	CS300	FLANGED NOZZLE		
N-3	8"	CS300	FLANGED NOZZLE		
N-1	8"	CS300	ASSUMED NOZZ...		

- To remove filter, right-click the **Data** table and select **Remove Filter**.

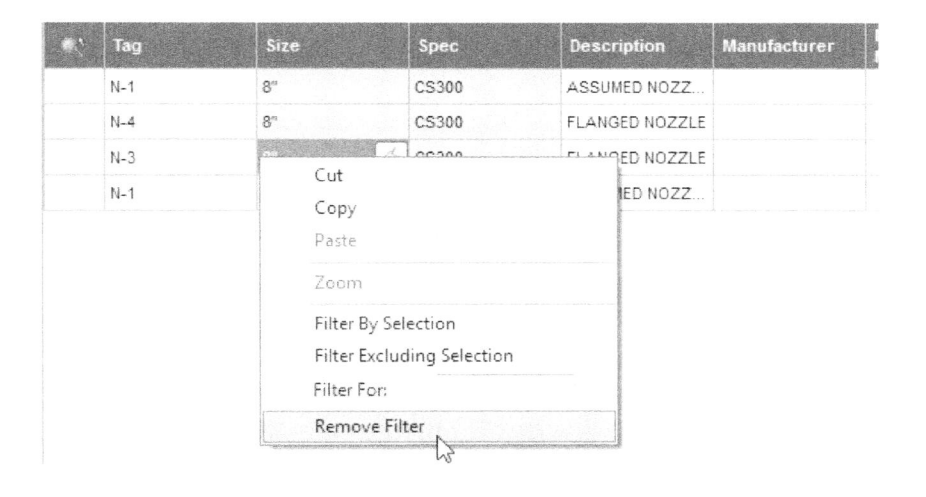

Tag	Size	Spec	Description	Manufacturer
N-1	8"	CS300	ASSUMED NOZZ...	
N-4	8"	CS300	FLANGED NOZZLE	
N-3		CS300	FLANGED NOZZLE	
N-1			ED NOZZ...	

[Context menu showing: Cut, Copy, Paste, Zoom, Filter By Selection, Filter Excluding Selection, Filter For:, Remove Filter]

- To filter by excluding the selection, right-click on the cell with '?' value and select **Filter Excluding Selection**.

#	Tag	Size	Spec	Description	Manufacture
	N-2	?	?	ASSUMED NOZZ...	
	N-2	10"	CS300	ASSUMED NOZZ...	
	N-1	?	?	ASSUMED NOZZ...	
	N-1	8"	CS300	ASSUMED NOZZ...	
▶	N-2	?	?	ASSUMED NOZZ...	
	N-4	8"	Cut	ZLE	
	N-1	?	Copy	...	
	N-6	10"	Paste	ZLE	
	N-3	8"	Zoom	ZLE	
	N-2	?	Filter By Selection	...	
	N-1	8"	Filter Excluding Selection	Z...	
	N-3	?	Filter For:	Z...	
	N-4	?	Remove Filter	Z...	
	N-1	?	?	FLANGED NOZZLE	

Now, you need to add some information to the Data table.

- Add the manufacturer information in the **Manufacturer** column.

#	Tag	Size	Spec	Description	Manufacturer	Model Number
	N-2	10"	CS300	ASSUMED NOZZ...		
▶	N-1	8"	CS300	ASSUMED NOZZ...	Bluepoint	
	N-4	8"	CS300	FLANGED NOZZLE		
	N-6	10"	CS300	FLANGED NOZZLE		
	N-3	8"	CS300	FLANGED NOZZLE		
	N-1	8"	CS300	ASSUMED NOZZ...		

- Hide the empty columns by clicking the **Hide Blank Columns** button on the **Data Manager** toolbar.

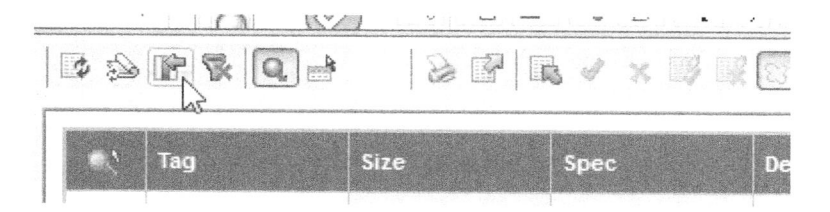

Exporting the Data

- Export the data by clicking the **Export** button on the **Data Manager** toolbar.

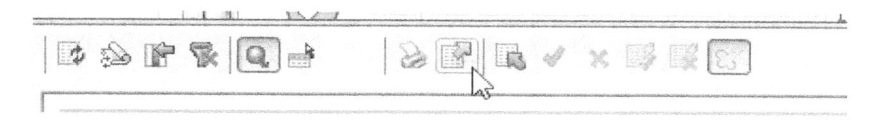

The **Export Data** dialog box appears.

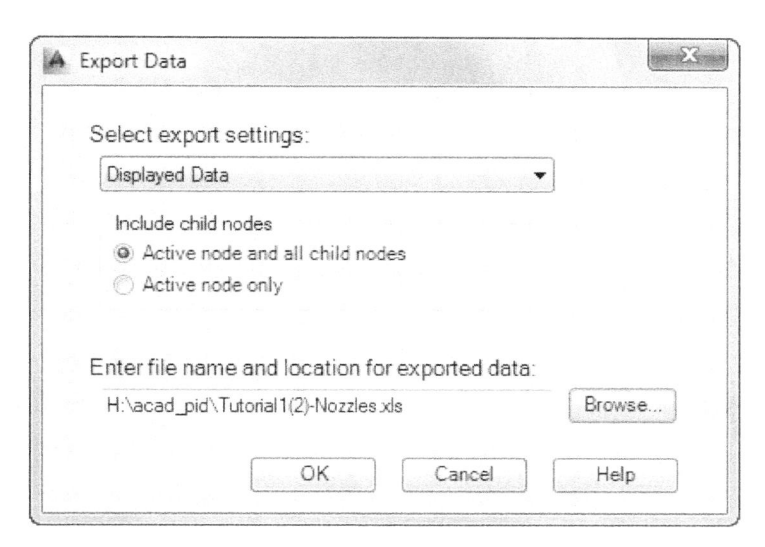

- Click the **Active node only** option under **Include child nodes**.

- Click the **Browse** button and specify the location of the export file.

AutoCAD P&ID Tutorial

- In the **Export To** dialog box, specify the file type using the **File Type** drop-down.

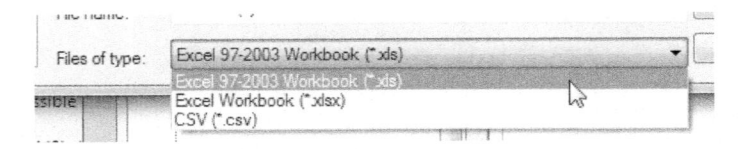

Files of type:	Excel 97-2003 Workbook (*.xls)
	Excel 97-2003 Workbook (*.xls)
	Excel Workbook (*.xlsx)
	CSV (*.csv)

- Click the **Save** button

- Click **OK** to export the data.

- Browse to the location of the exported file and open it.

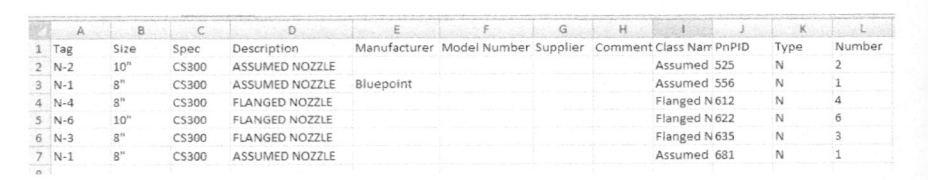

	A	B	C	D	E	F	G	H	I	J	K	L
1	Tag	Size	Spec	Description	Manufacturer	Model Number	Supplier	Comment	Class Nam	PnPID	Type	Number
2	N-2	10"	CS300	ASSUMED NOZZLE					Assumed	525	N	2
3	N-1	8"	CS300	ASSUMED NOZZLE	Bluepoint				Assumed	556	N	1
4	N-4	8"	CS300	FLANGED NOZZLE					Flanged N	612	N	4
5	N-6	10"	CS300	FLANGED NOZZLE					Flanged N	622	N	6
6	N-3	8"	CS300	FLANGED NOZZLE					Flanged N	635	N	3
7	N-1	8"	CS300	ASSUMED NOZZLE					Assumed	681	N	1

- Enter the **Manufacturer** information.

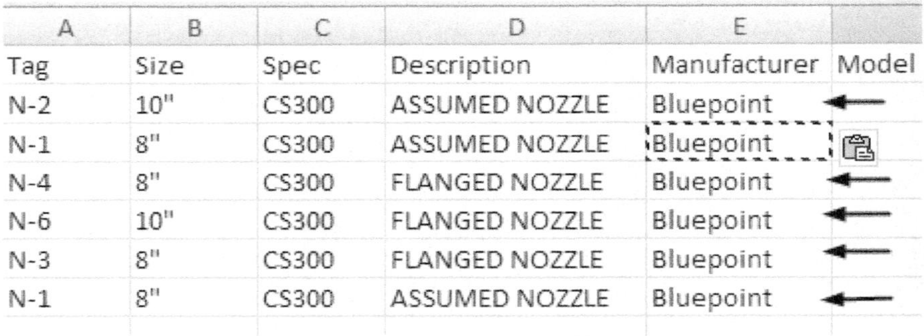

A	B	C	D	E	
Tag	Size	Spec	Description	Manufacturer	Model
N-2	10"	CS300	ASSUMED NOZZLE	Bluepoint	
N-1	8"	CS300	ASSUMED NOZZLE	Bluepoint	
N-4	8"	CS300	FLANGED NOZZLE	Bluepoint	
N-6	10"	CS300	FLANGED NOZZLE	Bluepoint	
N-3	8"	CS300	FLANGED NOZZLE	Bluepoint	
N-1	8"	CS300	ASSUMED NOZZLE	Bluepoint	

- Save the spreadsheet.

Now, you need to import the spreadsheet.

- Click the **Import** button on the **Data Manager** toolbar.

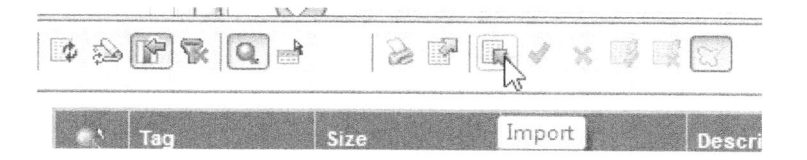

The AutoCAD P&ID message box appears.

- Click OK.

- In the **Import From** dialog box, browse to the location of the spreadsheet and double click to open the file.

The **Import Data** dialog box appears.

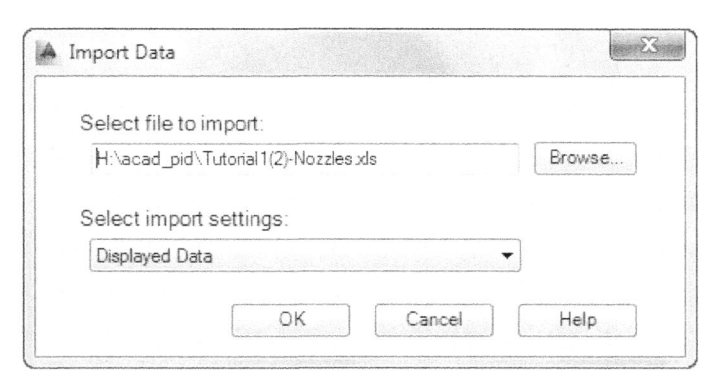

- Click **OK** to import the data.

AutoCAD P&ID Tutorial

You will notice that all the edited cells are displayed in yellow color.

Tag	Size	Spec	Description	Manufacturer	Class Nan
N-2	10"	CS300	ASSUMED NOZZ...	Bluepoint	Assumed N
N-1	8"	CS300	ASSUMED NOZZ...	Bluepoint	Assumed N
N-4	8"	CS300	FLANGED NOZZLE	Bluepoint	Flanged No
N-6	10"	CS300	FLANGED NOZZLE	Bluepoint	Flanged No
N-3	8"	CS300	FLANGED NOZZLE	Bluepoint	Flanged No
N-1	8"	CS300	ASSUMED NOZZ...	Bluepoint	Assumed N

- Click the fifth row of the first column; the drawing will be zoomed to the related nozzle.

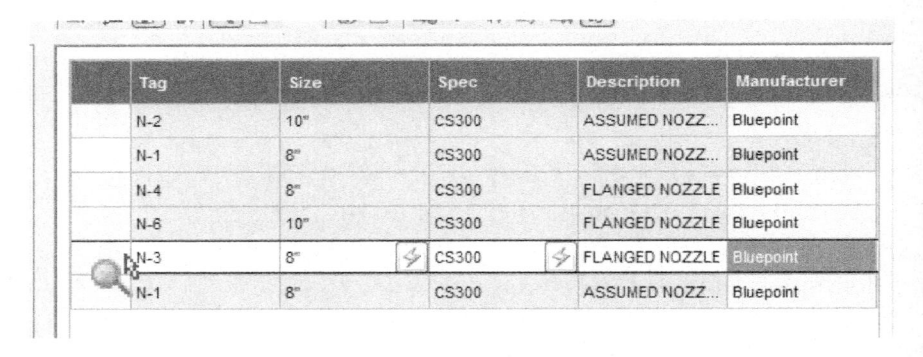

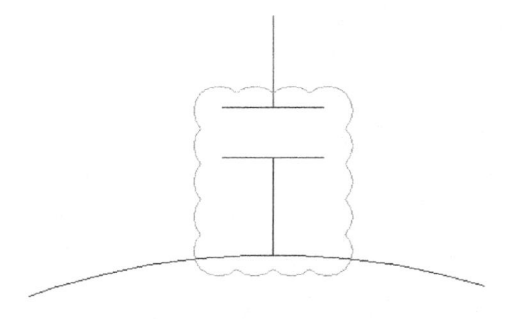

Tag	Size	Spec	Description	Manufacturer
N-2	10"	CS300	ASSUMED NOZZ...	Bluepoint
N-1	8"	CS300	ASSUMED NOZZ...	Bluepoint
N-4	8"	CS300	FLANGED NOZZLE	Bluepoint
N-6	10"	CS300	FLANGED NOZZLE	Bluepoint
N-3	8"	CS300	FLANGED NOZZLE	Bluepoint
N-1	8"	CS300	ASSUMED NOZZ...	Bluepoint

You will notice that the nozzle is marked with a revision cloud. Also, all the nozzles whose information is changed will be marked with revision clouds.

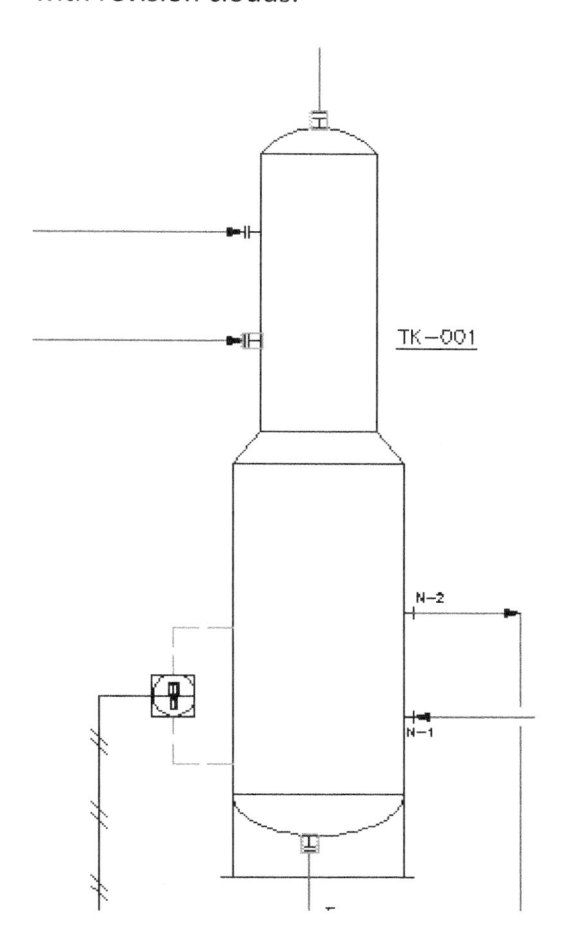

- Click the **Accept** button on the **Data Manager** toolbar to accept the edited value.

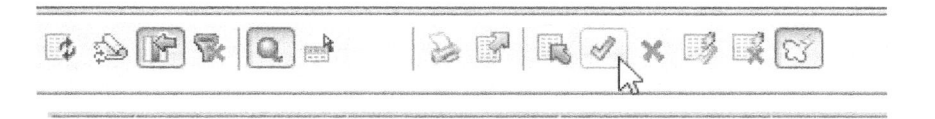

- Click the **Accept All** button to accept all the edited values.

Adding Annotations using the Data Manager

- Click **Equipment** in the **Class** tree; the equipment data is displayed.

- In the Data table, click in the **Description** cell of the P-001 component.

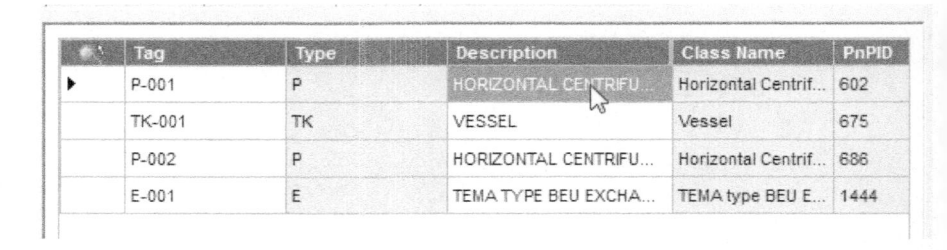

Tag	Type	Description	Class Name	PnPID
P-001	P	HORIZONTAL CENTRIFU...	Horizontal Centrif...	602
TK-001	TK	VESSEL	Vessel	675
P-002	P	HORIZONTAL CENTRIFU...	Horizontal Centrif...	686
E-001	E	TEMA TYPE BEU EXCHA...	TEMA type BEU E...	1444

- Drag and place the description below the centrifugal pump.

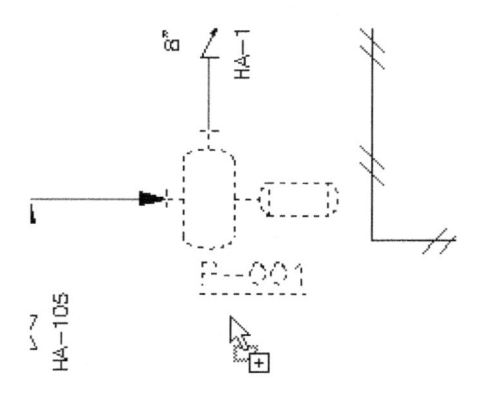

AutoCAD P&ID Tutorial

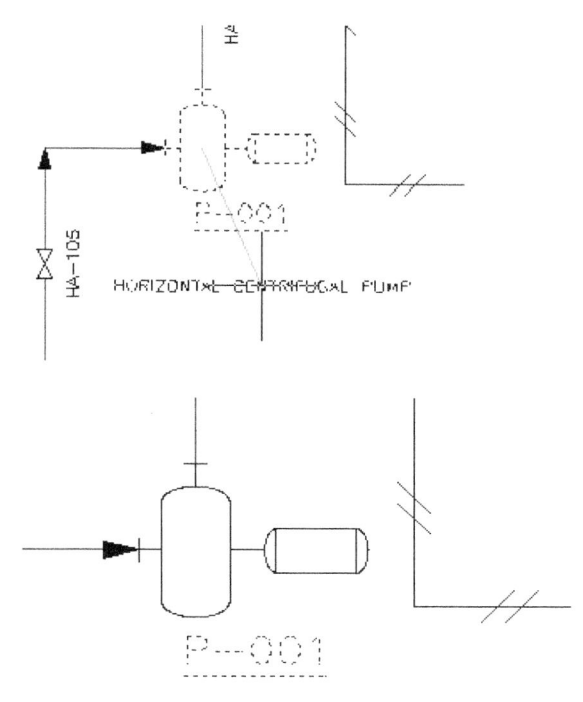

HORIZONTAL CENTRIFUGAL PUMP

- Save and close all the files.

Tutorial 5 (Defining a new Class)

In this tutorial, you will create a block of a symbol and add it to the category list of the project.

- Start a new drawing by clicking the **New** button on the Quick Access toolbar.

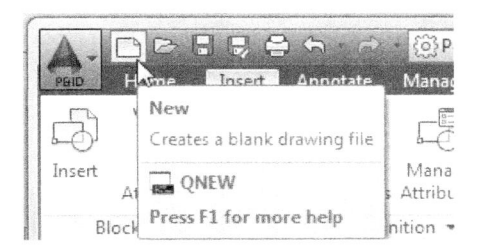

AutoCAD P&ID Tutorial

- Create the symbol shown below.

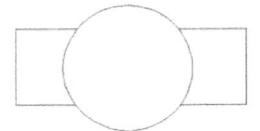

- Select all the entities of the symbol.

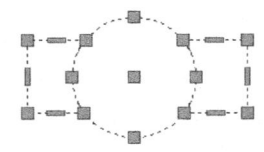

- Click the **Create Block** button on the **Block Definition** panel of the **Insert** tab.

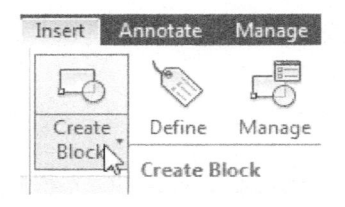

- In the **Block Definition** dialog box, enter **Vacuum Pump** in the **Name** edit box.

- Click the **Pick Point** button on the **Block Definition** dialog box.

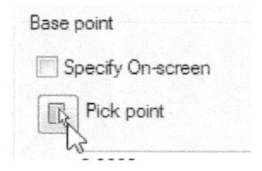

- Select the center point of the circle as the base point.

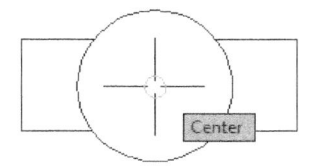

- Click the **OK** button to create the block.

- Save the file with the name **Vaccum_Pump.dwg** in the **TUTORIAL PROJECT** folder.

Next, you need to define a new class using the **Project Setup** dialog box.

- Open the **TUTORIAL PROJECT** project, if not already opened.

To open a project, click the **Open** option on the drop-down in the **Project Manager**.

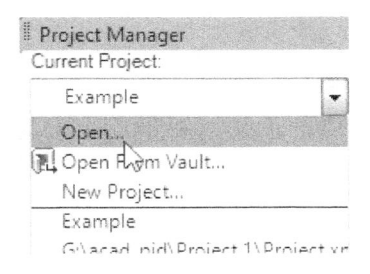

Browse to the **TUTORIAL PROJECT** folder and double-click on the **Project.xml** file.

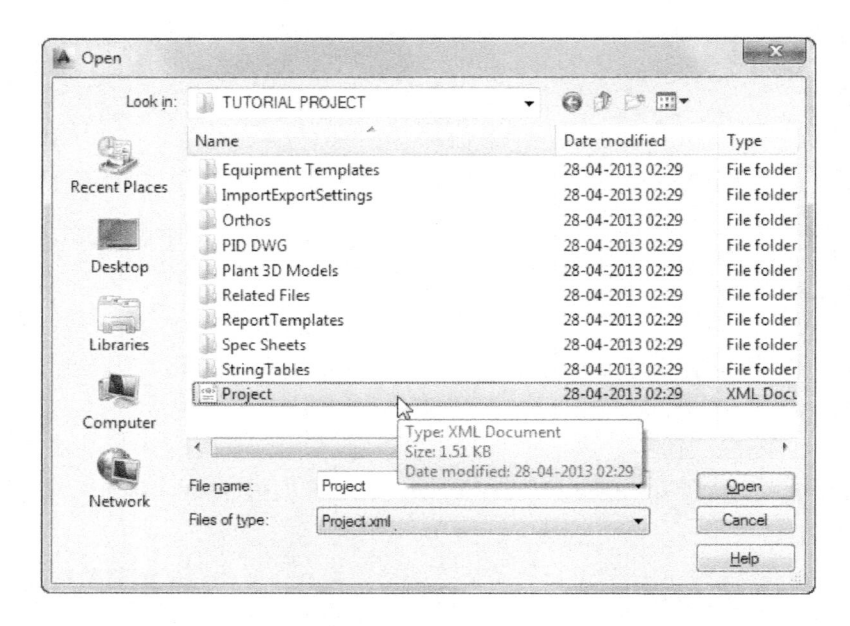

- Click the **Project Setup** button from the **Project** drop-down in the **Project** panel.

The **Project Setup** dialog box appears.

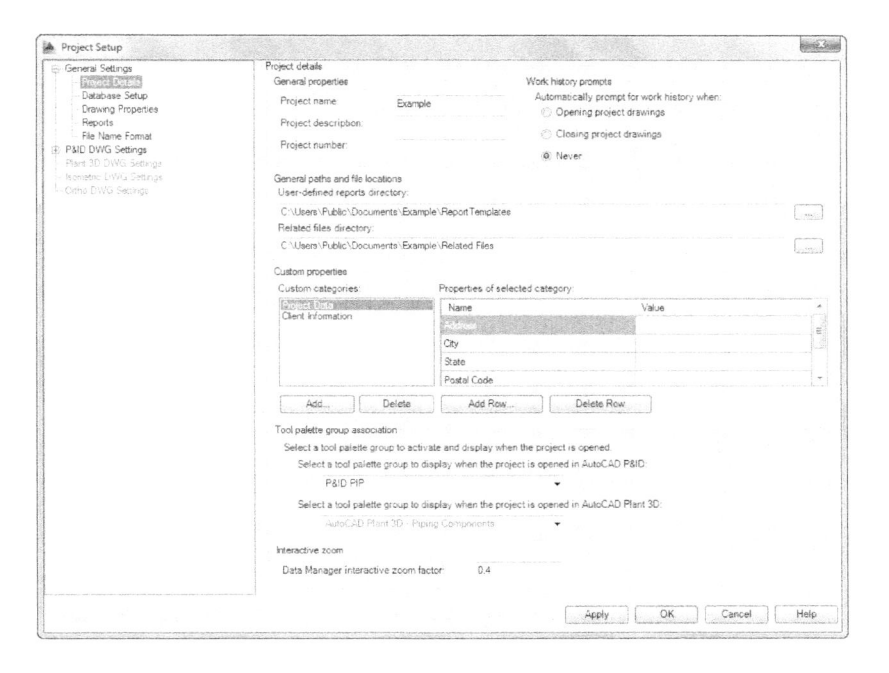

- Expand the **P&ID DWG Settings** node.

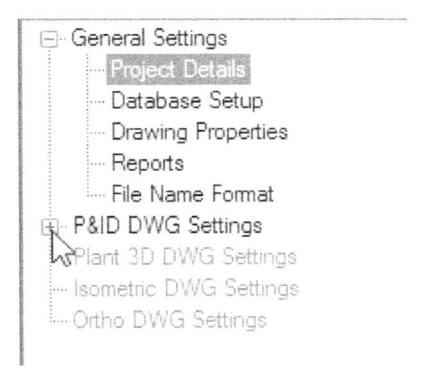

- In the **P&ID DWG Settings**, expand **Engineering Items > Equipment > Pumps**.

- Right-click on **Pumps** and click **New**.

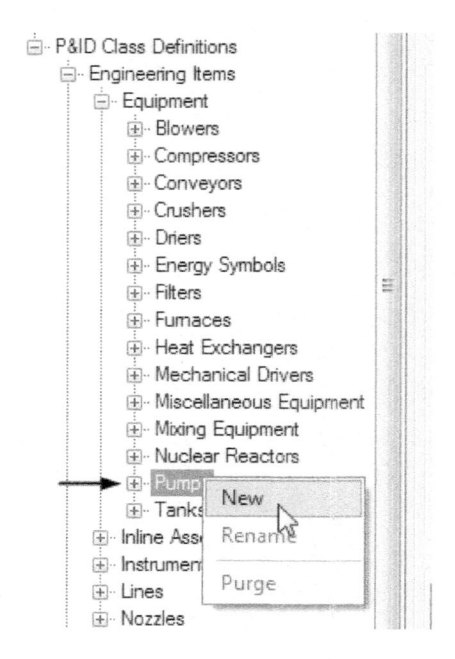

```
P&ID Class Definitions
  Engineering Items
    Equipment
      Blowers
      Compressors
      Conveyors
      Crushers
      Driers
      Energy Symbols
      Filters
      Furnaces
      Heat Exchangers
      Mechanical Drivers
      Miscellaneous Equipment
      Mixing Equipment
      Nuclear Reactors
      Pumps        New
      Tanks        Rename
    Inline Asse
    Instrumen    Purge
    Lines
    Nozzles
```

- In the **Create Class** dialog box, enter **Vacuum_Pump** in the **Class Name** field.

- Enter **Vacuum Pump** in the **Display Name of the Class** field.

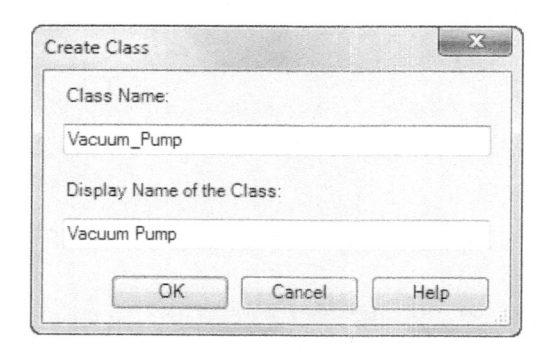

Create Class

Class Name:
Vacuum_Pump

Display Name of the Class:
Vacuum Pump

OK   Cancel   Help

- Click the **OK** button.

The new class is displayed under the **Pumps** list.

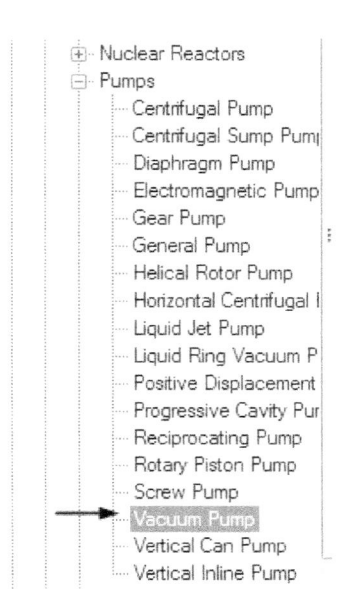

```
⊕ Nuclear Reactors
⊟ Pumps
    Centrifugal Pump
    Centrifugal Sump Pump
    Diaphragm Pump
    Electromagnetic Pump
    Gear Pump
    General Pump
    Helical Rotor Pump
    Horizontal Centrifugal l
    Liquid Jet Pump
    Liquid Ring Vacuum P
    Positive Displacement
    Progressive Cavity Pur
    Reciprocating Pump
    Rotary Piston Pump
    Screw Pump
 →  Vacuum Pump
    Vertical Can Pump
    Vertical Inline Pump
```

- Select the **Vacuum Pump** class from the list and click the **Add Symbols** button under **Class Settings: Vacuum Pump**.

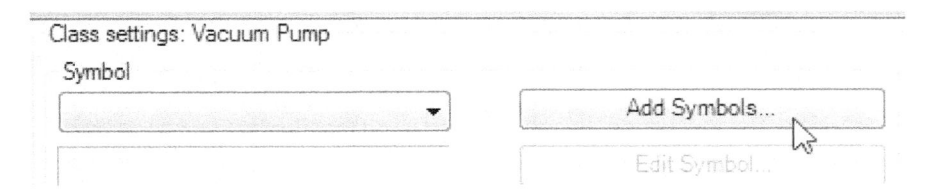

Class settings: Vacuum Pump
Symbol

[▼]   [Add Symbols...]
[   ]   [Edit Symbol...]

The **Add Symbols** dialog box appears.

- In this dialog box, click the **Browse** button next to the **Selected Drawings** field.

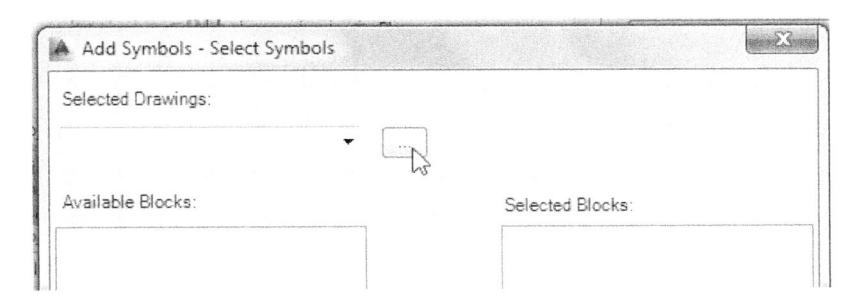

Add Symbols - Select Symbols
Selected Drawings:
[▼] [...]

Available Blocks: Selected Blocks:

- In the **Select Block Drawing** dialog box, browse to the **TUTORIAL PROJECT** folder and double-click on the **Vacuum_Pump.dwg**.

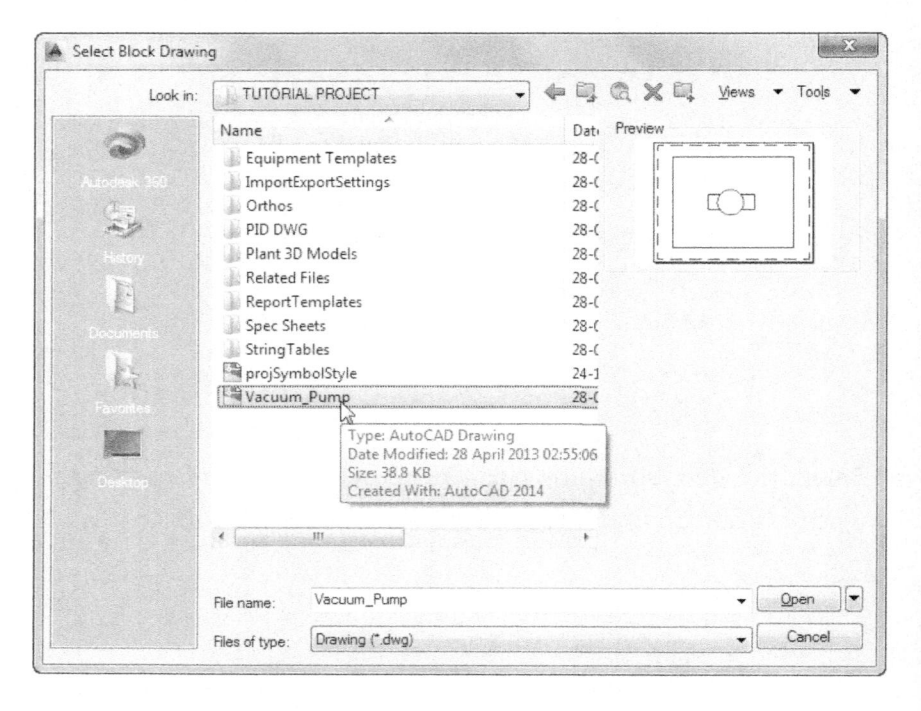

- In the **Add Symbols** dialog box, select **Vacuum_Pump** from the **Available Blocks** list and click the **Add** button.

- Click the **Next** button.

The **Add Symbols-Edit Symbol Settings** dialog box appears.

AutoCAD P&ID Tutorial

Add Symbols - Edit Symbol Settings

Selected Blocks: Vacuum Pump

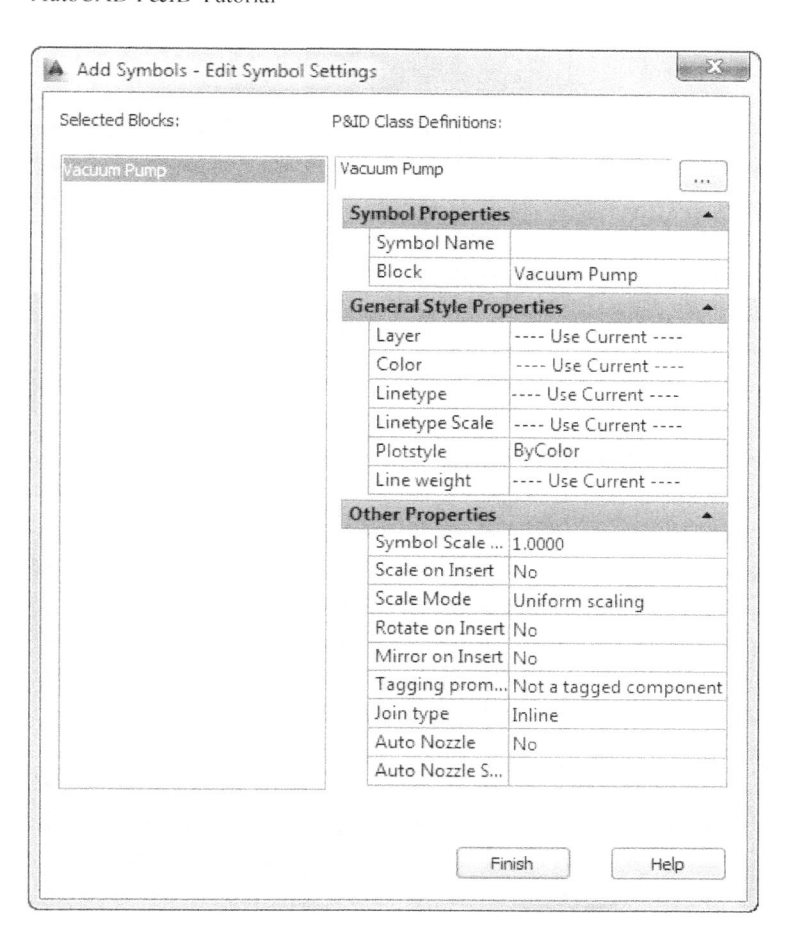

P&ID Class Definitions: Vacuum Pump

Symbol Properties

Symbol Name	
Block	Vacuum Pump

General Style Properties

Layer	---- Use Current ----
Color	---- Use Current ----
Linetype	---- Use Current ----
Linetype Scale	---- Use Current ----
Plotstyle	ByColor
Line weight	---- Use Current ----

Other Properties

Symbol Scale ...	1.0000
Scale on Insert	No
Scale Mode	Uniform scaling
Rotate on Insert	No
Mirror on Insert	No
Tagging prom...	Not a tagged component
Join type	Inline
Auto Nozzle	No
Auto Nozzle S...	

[Finish] [Help]

- Enter **Vacuum Pump** in the **Symbol Name** edit box.

- Specify the other properties as shown below.

Add Symbols - Edit Symbol Settings	
Selected Blocks:	P&ID Class Definitions:
Vacuum Pump	Vacuum Pump

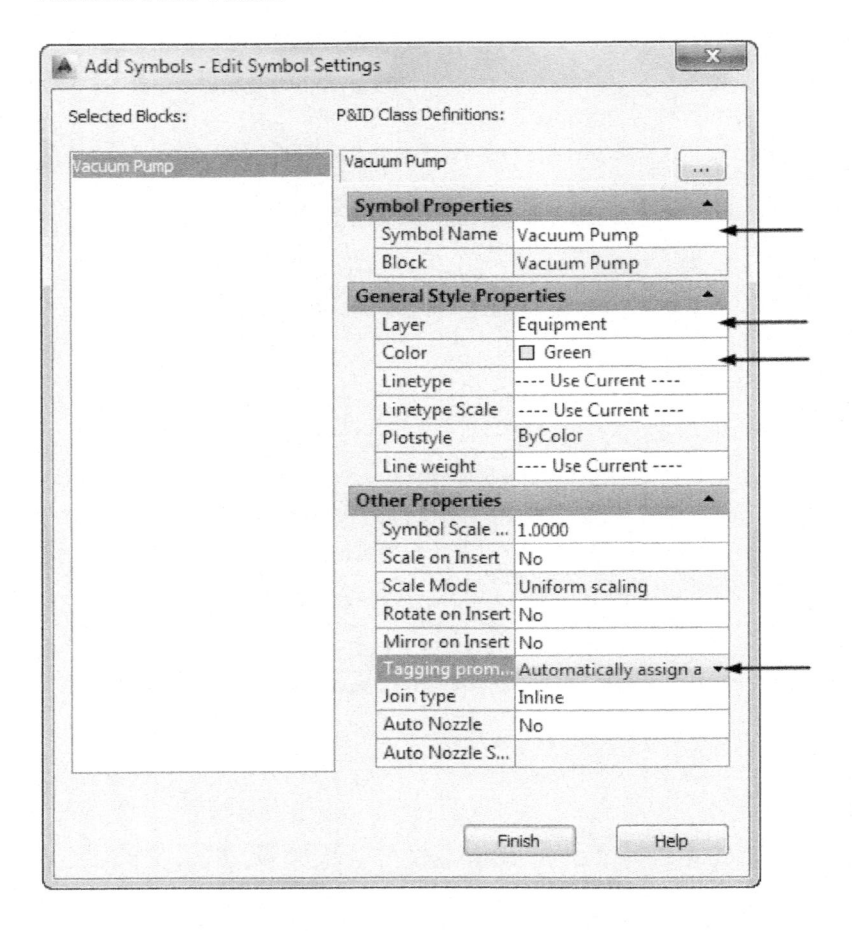

Symbol Properties	
Symbol Name	Vacuum Pump
Block	Vacuum Pump
General Style Properties	
Layer	Equipment
Color	☐ Green
Linetype	---- Use Current ----
Linetype Scale	---- Use Current ----
Plotstyle	ByColor
Line weight	---- Use Current ----
Other Properties	
Symbol Scale ...	1.0000
Scale on Insert	No
Scale Mode	Uniform scaling
Rotate on Insert	No
Mirror on Insert	No
Tagging prom...	Automatically assign a
Join type	Inline
Auto Nozzle	No
Auto Nozzle S...	

- Click the **Finish** button; the symbol will be added to the list.

- Click the **Edit Block** button under **Class settings: Vacuum Pump**.

AutoCAD P&ID Tutorial

Class settings: Vacuum Pump
Symbol

[Vacuum Pump ▼]   [Add Symbols...]
                  [Edit Symbol...]
                  [Remove Symbol...]
                  [Edit Block...]   ←
                  [Add to Tool Palette...]

Properties

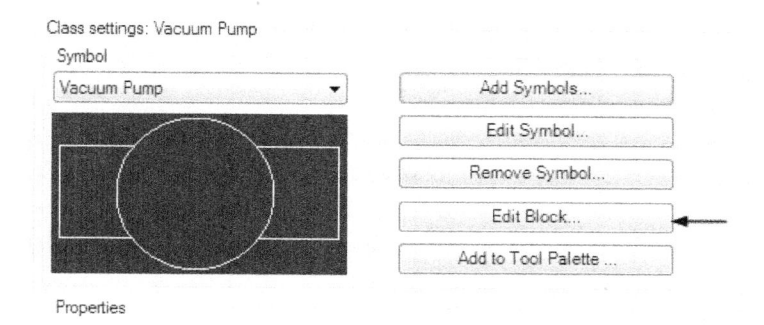

The block editor will be opened.

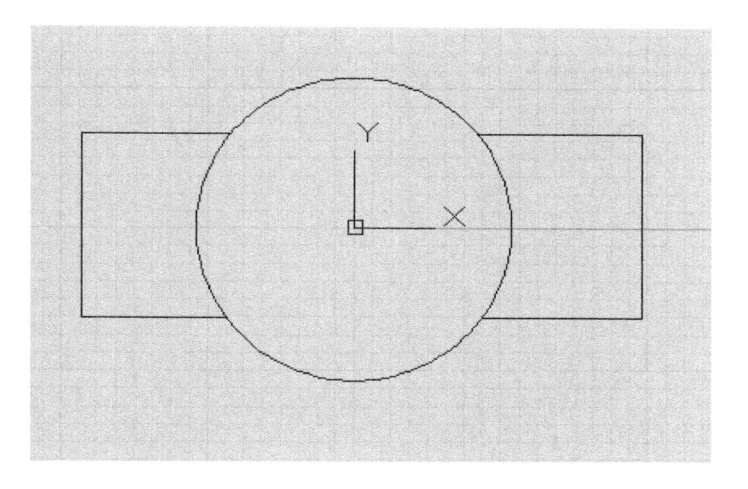

- Select the **Parameters** tab from the **Block Authoring Palettes** tool palette.

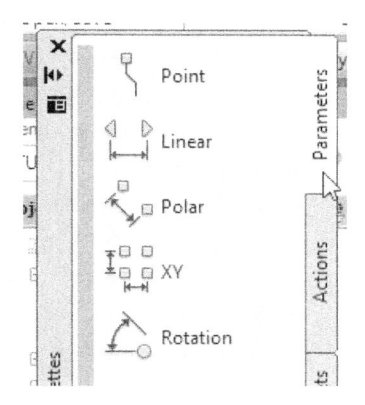

Point
Linear
Polar
XY
Rotation

- Select the **Point** button from the tool palette.

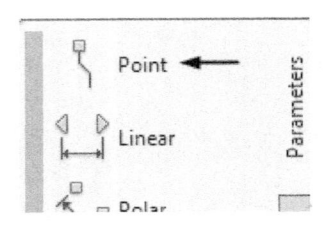

- Press and hold the **Shift** key and right-click to display the shortcut menu.

- Click **Midpoint** on the shortcut menu.

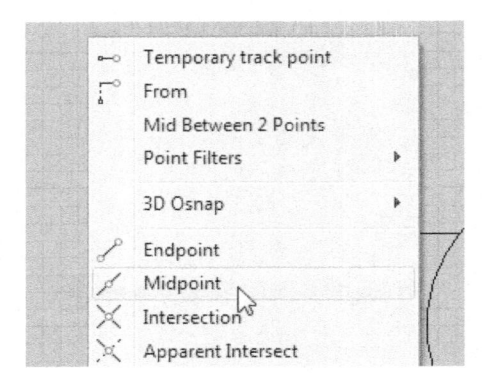

- Select the midpoint of the left vertical line.

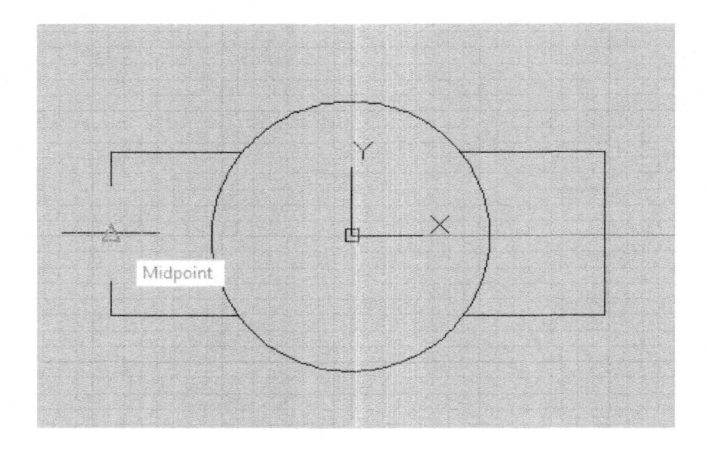

AutoCAD P&ID Tutorial

- Move the cursor toward left and click.

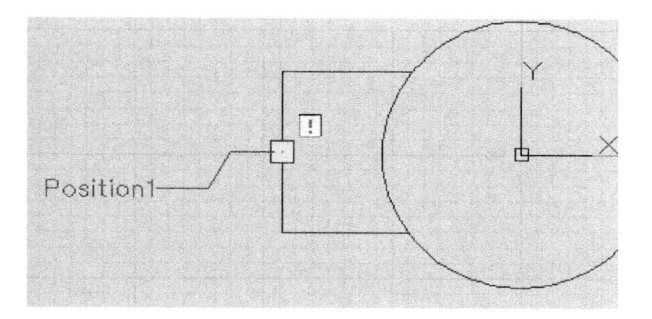

- Similarly, add another point on the right vertical line.

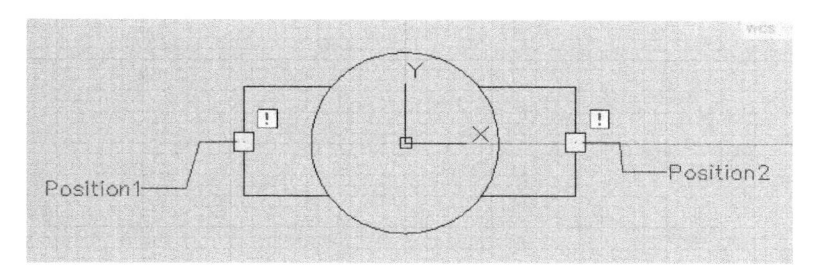

- Click on the yellow grip displayed on the left point and invoke the **Properties** palette.

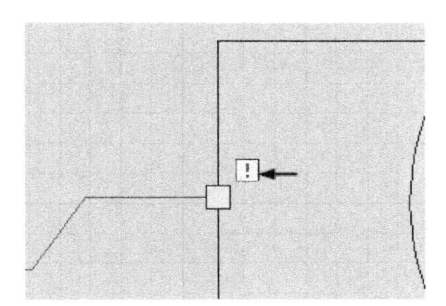

- In the **Properties** palette, under the **Property Labels**, enter **AttachmentPoint1** in the **Position name** field.

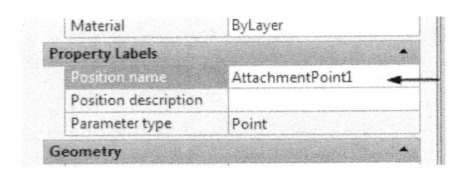

- Similarly, specify the **Position name** of the second point as **AttachmentPoint2**.

- Click the **Save Block** button on the **Open/Save** panel.

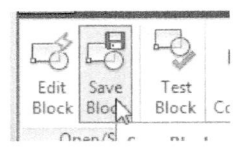

- Click the **Close Block Editor** button.

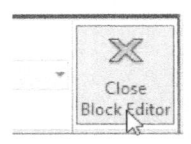

Next, you need to add this symbol to the tool palette.

- Click the **Add to Tool Palette** button under **Class Settings: Vacuum Pump** in the **Project Setup** dialog box.

- Click **OK**.

The **Vacuum Pump** will be added to the tool palette.

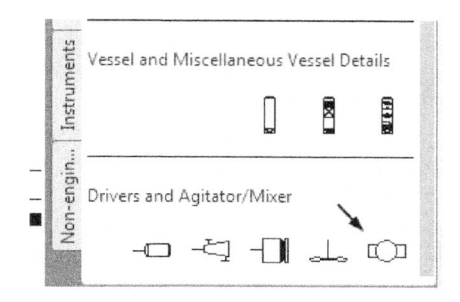

Adding Annotations to the Symbol

Now, you need to add annotations to the symbol

- To add annotations to the symbol, make sure that **Equipment tag** is selected in the drop-down available under **Annotation**.

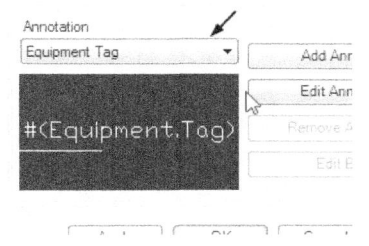

- Click the **Add Annotation** button under **Annotation** on the **Project Setup** dialog box; the **Symbol Settings** dialog box appears.

- Enter **New Equipment tag** in the **Symbol Name** field under the **Symbol Properties** group.

- Make sure that **Equipment Tag_block** is displayed in the **Block** field.

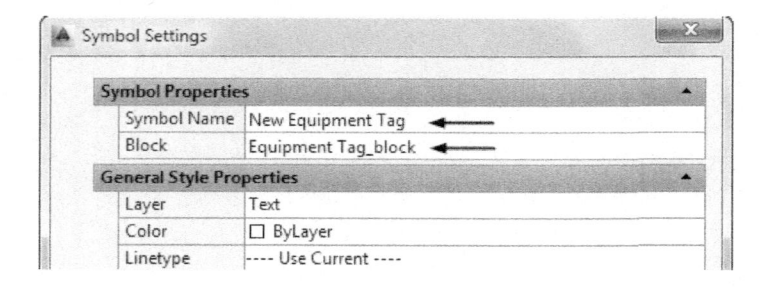

- Click **OK**.

Now you need to assign a format to the annotation.

- Click the **Edit Block** button under **Annotation** on the **Project Setup** dialog box.

The **Block Editor** will be opened.

- Click the **Assign Format** button on the **Annotation** toolbar.

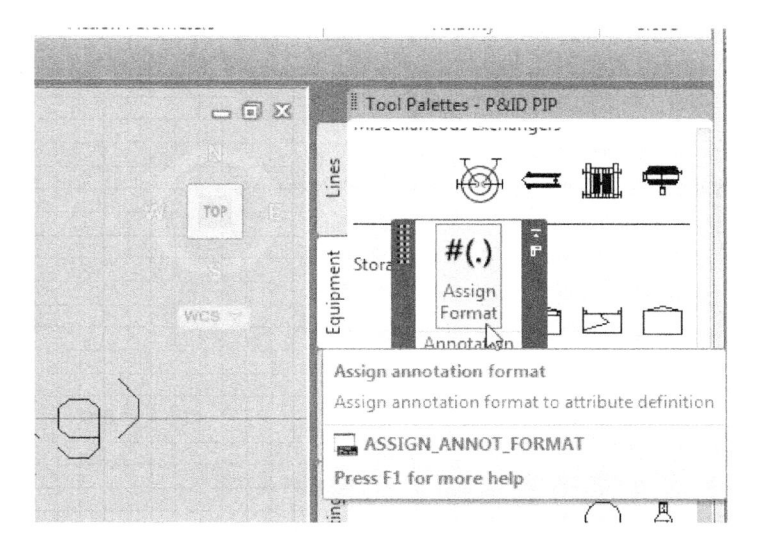

- Select the **#(Equipment Tag)** attribute from the graphics window; the Assign **Annotation Format** dialog box appears.

- Click the **Select Class Properties** button on the **Assign Annotation Format** dialog box.

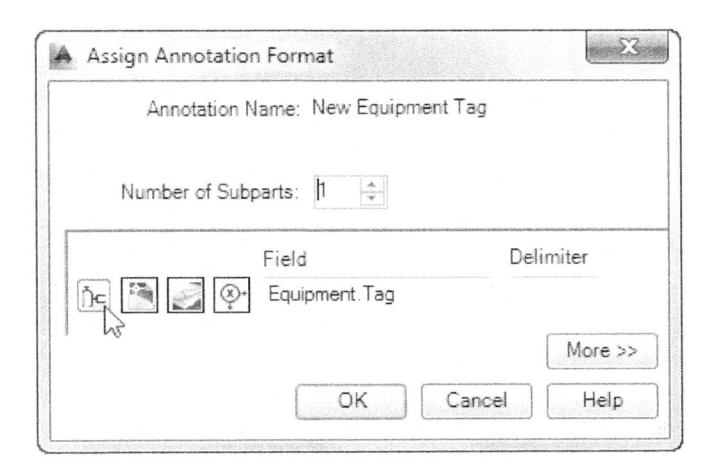

The **Select Class Property** dialog box appears.

- In the **Select Class Properties** dialog box, select **Engineering Items > Equipment**.

- Select **Equipment Spec** from the **Property** list.

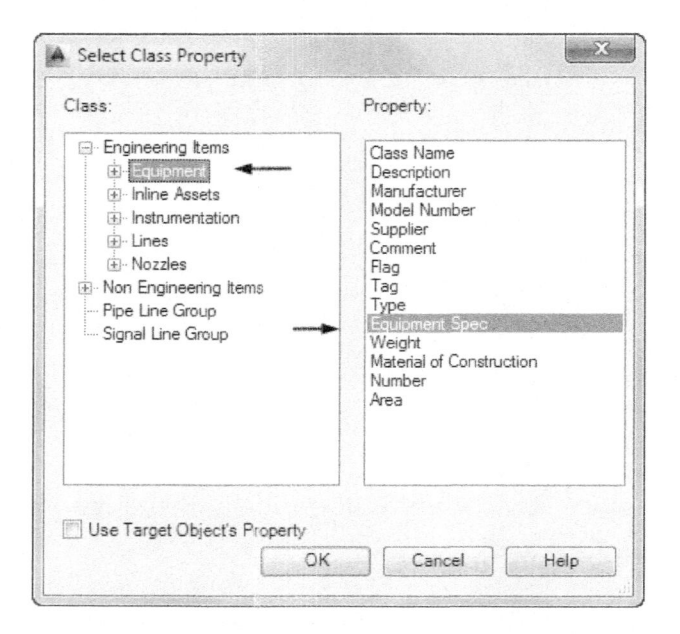

- Click **OK** on the **Select Class Property** dialog box.

- Click **OK** on the **Assign Annotation Format** dialog box.

- Close the **Block Editor** and save the changes made.

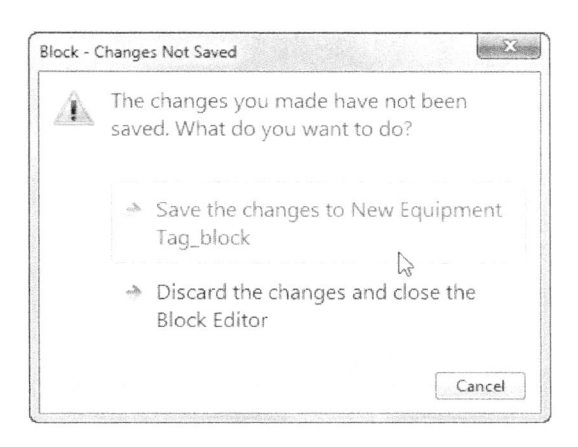

- In the **Project Setup** dialog box, make sure that **Vacuum Pump** is selected in the **Category** list.

- Select **New Equipment Tag** as the **Default Value** for the **AnnotationStyleName**.

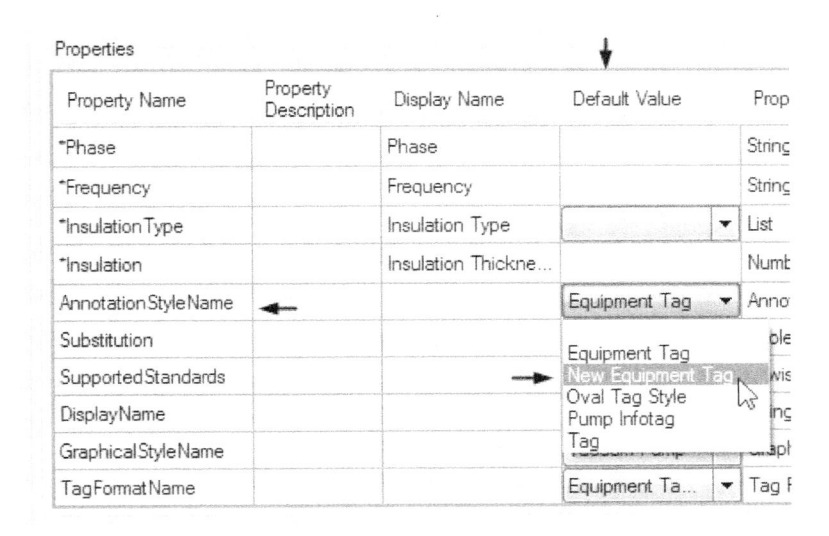

- Click the **Apply** button.

- Click the **OK** button.

Tutorial 6 (Generate Reports)

In this tutorial, you generate reports using the Report Creator.

- To start the Report Creator, click **Start > Program Files > Autodesk > AutoCAD P&ID 2014 > AutoCAD Plant Report Creator 2014**.

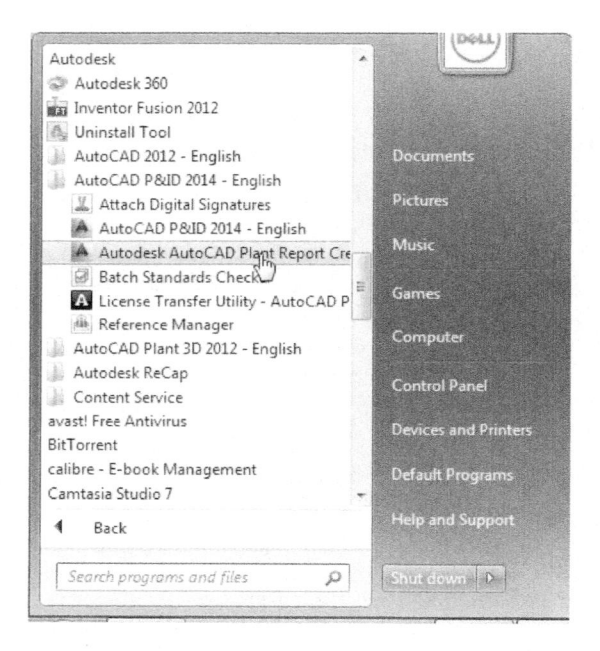

The **Settings** dialog box appears.

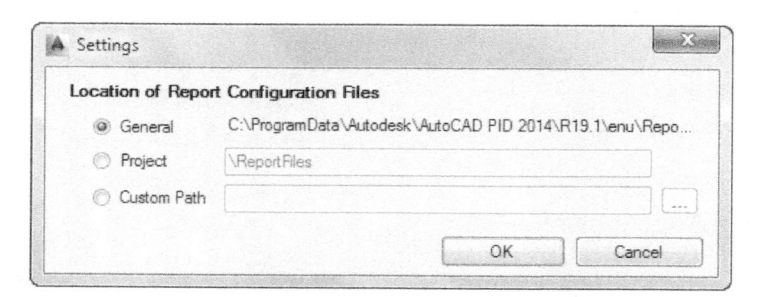

In this dialog box, you can specify the location of the report files. You can use the **General** option to specify the default location. The **Project** option is used to specify the report file location in the **ReportFiles** folder under the current project directory. You can also use the **Custom Path** option to specify the custom location for the report files.

- Select the **General** option from the **Settings** dialog box and click **OK**.

- Click the **Open** option on the **Project** drop-down in the **Autodesk AutoCAD Plant Report Creator**.

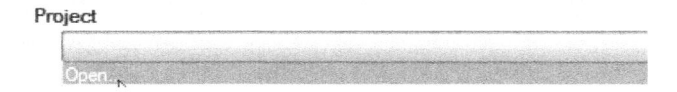

- Browse to location ....**TUTORIAL PROJECT\Project.xml**.

- Click the **Open** button to the set the project for generating the reports.

- Select **Linelist** from the **Report Configuration** drop-down.

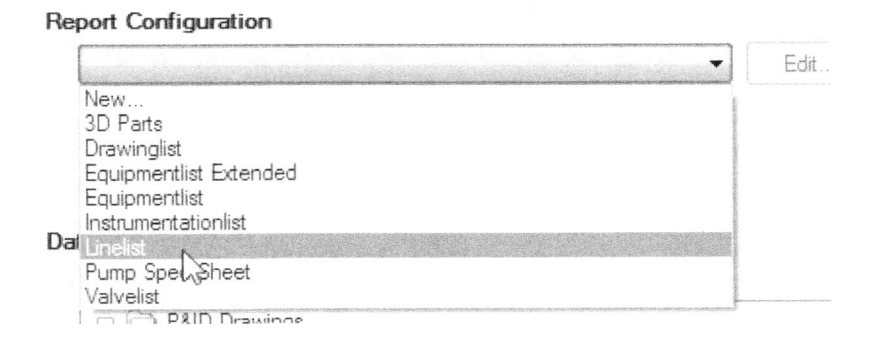

- Click the **Preview** button; the **Preview** window appears.

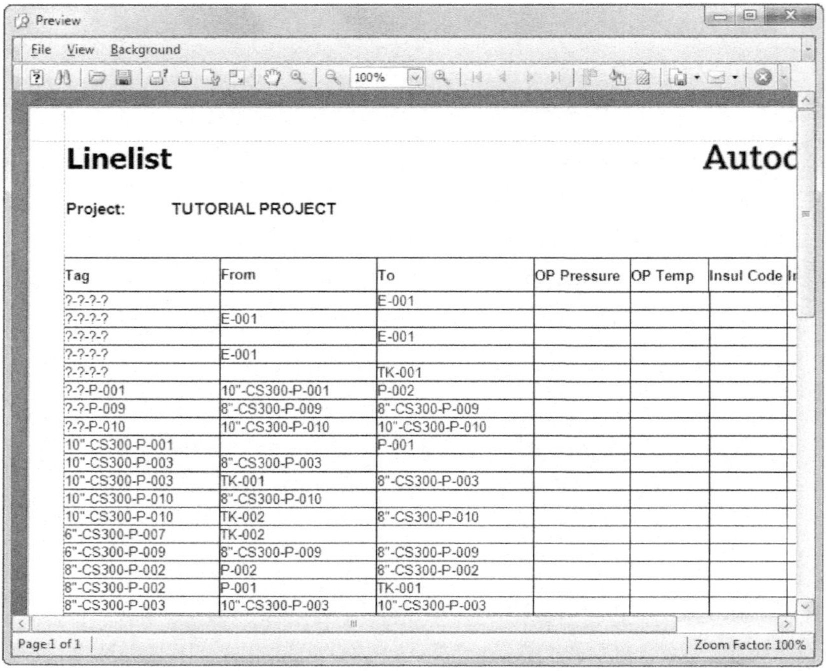
Preview
File View Background
100%
Linelist
Autoc
Project: TUTORIAL PROJECT
Tag From To OP Pressure OP Temp Insul Code
?-?-?-? E-001
?-?-?-? E-001
?-?-?-? E-001
?-?-?-? E-001
?-?-?-? TK-001
?-?-P-001 10"-CS300-P-001 P-002
?-?-P-009 8"-CS300-P-009 8"-CS300-P-009
?-?-P-010 10"-CS300-P-010 10"-CS300-P-010
10"-CS300-P-001 P-001
10"-CS300-P-003 8"-CS300-P-003
10"-CS300-P-003 TK-001 8"-CS300-P-003
10"-CS300-P-010 8"-CS300-P-010
10"-CS300-P-010 TK-002 8"-CS300-P-010
6"-CS300-P-007 TK-002
6"-CS300-P-009 8"-CS300-P-009 8"-CS300-P-009
8"-CS300-P-002 P-002 8"-CS300-P-002
8"-CS300-P-002 P-001 TK-001
8"-CS300-P-003 10"-CS300-P-003 10"-CS300-P-003
Page 1 of 1
Zoom Factor: 100%

Using the options in this window, you can modify the display of the report by changing the background color, page setup and so on. You can also specify the export format of the report.

You can also save the changes as a template. Click **Export Document > PDF File** on the Toolbar; the **PDF Export Options** dialog box appears. Click the **OK** button; the **Save As** dialog box appears. Specify the location of the template file.

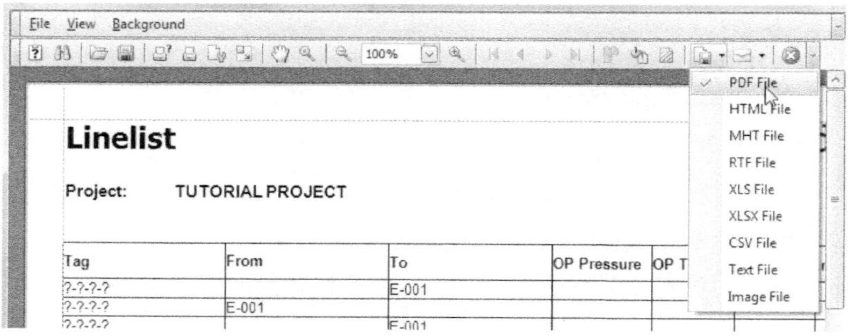
File View Background
100%
PDF File
HTML File
MHT File
RTF File
XLS File
XLSX File
CSV File
Text File
Image File
Linelist
Project: TUTORIAL PROJECT
Tag From To OP Pressure OP T
?-?-?-? E-001
?-?-?-? E-001

- Close the **Preview** window.

- Click **Print/Export**; the **PDF Export Options** dialog box appears.

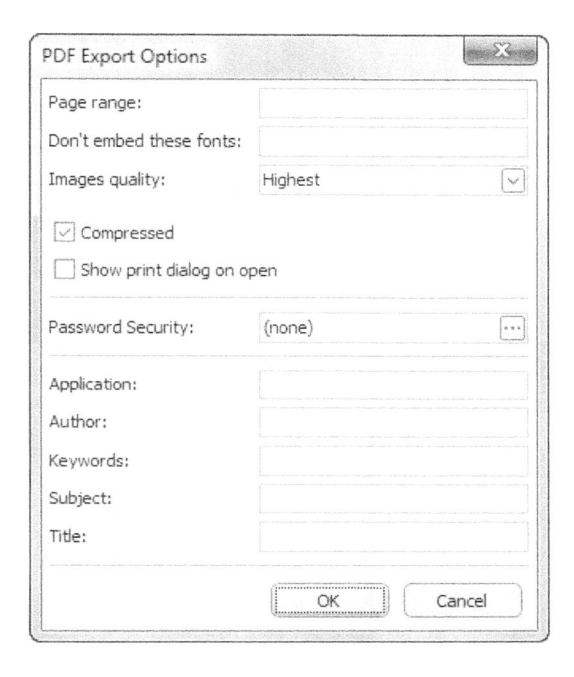

- Click the **OK** button; the **Export Results** dialog box appears.

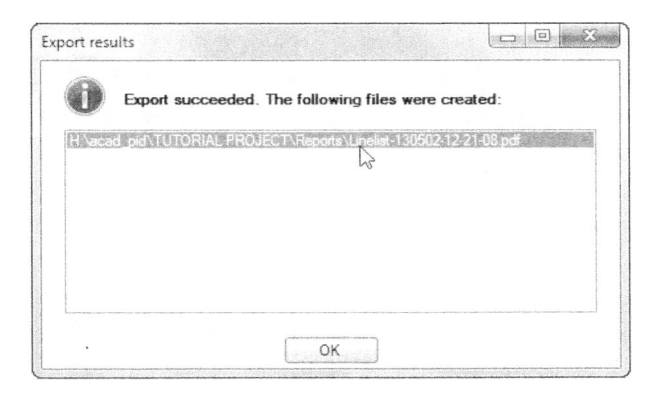

- Double-click on the listed PDF file in the **Export results** dialog box; the PDF file will be opened.

- View the report in the PDF file.

Linelist

Project: TUTORIAL PROJECT

Tag	From	To	OP Pressure	OP Temp	Insul Code	Insul Thick
?-?-?-?		E-001				
?-?-?-?	E-001					
?-?-?-?		E-001				
?-?-?-?	E-001					
?-?-?-?		TK-001				
?-?-P-001	10"-CS300-P-001	P-002				
?-?-P-009	8"-CS300-P-009	8"-CS300-P-009				
?-?-P-010	10"-CS300-P-010	10"-CS300-P-010				
10"-CS300-P-001		P-001				
10"-CS300-P-003	8"-CS300-P-003					
10"-CS300-P-003	TK-001	8"-CS300-P-003				
10"-CS300-P-010	8"-CS300-P-010					
10"-CS300-P-010	TK-002	8"-CS300-P-010				
6"-CS300-P-007	TK-002					
6"-CS300-P-009	8"-CS300-P-009	8"-CS300-P-009				
8"-CS300-P-002	P-002	8"-CS300-P-002				
8"-CS300-P-002	P-001	TK-001				
8"-CS300-P-003	10"-CS300-P-003	10"-CS300-P-003				
8"-CS300-P-005		E-002				
8"-CS300-P-005	TK-001					
8"-CS300-P-006	E-002	TK-002				
8"-CS300-P-008	TK-002	P-003				
8"-CS300-P-009	6"-CS300-P-009					
8"-CS300-P-009	P-003	6"-CS300-P-009				

- Close all the files.

Printed in Great Britain
by Amazon